SAT 에세이
트레이너
Guidebook for SAT-Essay Writing

SAT/ACT 준비 대한민국 No.1
인터프렙의 또 하나의 베스트셀링
'트레이너' 시리즈!

초판 1쇄 발행 2019년 6월 3일

지은이 스티븐 박
감　수 정재환, 엄일석
펴낸이 장길수
펴낸곳 지식과감성°
출판등록 제2012-000081호

디자인 이현
편집 이현, 안영인
교정 나은비, 박솔빈
마케팅 고은빛

ISBN 979-11-6275-635-5(13740)
값 20,000원

ⓒ 인터프렙 2019 Printed in Korea

잘못된 책은 구입하신 곳에서 바꾸어 드립니다.
이 책의 전부 또는 일부 내용을 재사용하려면 사전에 저작권자와 펴낸곳의 동의를 받아야 합니다.

이 도서의 국립중앙도서관 출판예정도서목록(CIP)은 서지정보유통지원시스템
홈페이지(http://seoji.nl.go.kr)와 국가자료공동목록시스템(http://www.nl.go.kr/kolisnet)에서
이용하실 수 있습니다. (CIP제어번호 : CIP2019020582)

인터프렙 베스트셀링
'트레이너' 시리즈!

SAT 에세이 트레이너
Guidebook for SAT-Essay Writing
8-8-8

SAT-Essay 만점
8-8-8 성취를 위한 필승 트레이너!

인터프렙어학연구소
스티븐 박 저 / 정재환, 엄일석 감수

PREMIUM QUALITY
Premium Quality Trainer
Series From Interprep!
2019년 최신 경향 반영
SAT 에세이 영역
수험생 필독 베스트셀러
'No Nonsense'-Guaranteed!
GUARANTEED

✓ SAT 대한민국 #1 인터프렙 최고 강사진의 Know-how 전격 공개!
✓ 미국, 아시아 및 국내 명문대 입학이 목표인 입시생들의 필독서!
✓ 칼리지보드 채점자들의 심리를 꿰뚫는 고득점 전략!

www.interprep.co.kr

CONTENTS

PREFACE	6
Acknowledgements	8

Chapter 01   SAT Essay? – 그것이 알고 싶다!

- 문제 유형   10
- 채점 방식과 기준   10
- 어느 정도의 점수가 '좋은 점수'인가?   11

Chapter 02   SAT Essay 시험의 '성격'에 대한 이해   14

Chapter 03   지문에 대한 세부 요소별 분석

1. Evidences – 기법 / 전략적 요소   38
2. Reasoning – 논리적 요소   49
3. Stylistic elements – 스타일적인 요소   59

Chapter 04   템플릿을 준비하라 – Have your 'template' ready! + How to make your 'own' template.   76

Chapter 05	하지 말아야 할 것들 vs. 해야 할 것들 - What NOT to do vs. what to do!	
	Learning through the comparisons between some 'bad' essays and 'good' ones.	**92**

Chapter 06	Let's practice more - 6 SAT Essay practice tests with 'training guidelines'!	**114**

부록 (Appendix)	A. "A Crash Course in SAT-Essay!" (하루 또는 이틀밖에 준비 기간이 없을 경우 응급 처방식 준비!)	**150**
	B. Reasoning Pattern / Logical Thinking에 대한 정리	**154**
	C. **TOEFL Speaking & Writing Tips + Samples** (토플 고득점 성취를 위한 스피킹 및 라이팅 트레이너 Tips!)	**162**
	D. 연습용 답안지(복사용)	**185**

PREFACE

"이게 뭐예요?" "이거 리딩 지문 아닌가요?"
필자가 SAT-Essay 과정을 하면서 처음 수업에 참여하는 학생들에게 essay 지문을 나누어 주면 그들이 가끔 보이는 반응이다.

이러한 반응이 나오는 이유는 SAT-Essay가 좀 특이한 writing 시험 형식을 갖고 있어서이다. 사실 정확히 말하면 'Analysis & Writing'이 더 적절한 명칭이 될 것이다. 그러나 시험을 주관하는 Collegeboard에서는 아마도 혼란을 방지하기 위하여 new SAT로 변환하면서 그대로 명칭을 유지한 것 같다.

이렇게 생소한 형식을 가지고 있다 보니 많은 학생들이(ACT essay나 토플 essay, 그리고 나름 English composition 관련 학교 과정에서 좋은 성적을 받은 학생들까지도 포함하여) 이 부분에 대하여 상당히 어렵다고 느낀다. 사실 자신의 주장을 논리적으로 피력해야 하는 일반적 에세이 시험보다 쉬운데도 말이다.

이 책은 그러한 선입견을 가진 많은 학생들에게 SAT-Essay 대비 과정을 쉽게 풀어 주고자 저술되었다. New SAT가 아직 시행된 지 비교적 많지 않은 시간이 흐른 관례로 시중에는 현재 쓸데없이 심오한 Argumentative essay 작성이나 적절한 내용을 제시하거나 또는 판에 박힌 듯한 포맷(예: Aristotle의 'On Rhetoric'에 기초한 'Logos, Pathos, Ethos' 개념을 사용하여 분석과 작성을 하는, 그래서 자칫하면 외워서 쓴 것으로 오해받을 수 있는 방식과 표현)을 마치 정답인 듯 설명하는 준비서밖에 없는 실정이다.

Interprep SAT 강사진의 연구에 기초하여, 또한 현장 강의와 학생들의 점수 성취 과정에서의 피드백에 근거하여 이러한 어려울 수 있는 SAT 에세이를 쉽고 편하게 접근할 수 있도록 마련된 책이다. 준비할 것은 너무나도 많은데 시간은 턱없이 부족하다고 느끼는 많은 입시 준비생들에게 아주 효과적인 지침서가 될 것을 확신한다. 아무쪼록 이 책과 함께 효율적인 준비를 하여 원하는 SAT 점수를 각자의 스펙의 일부로 확보하여 각자 'Dream School'로 생각하는 대학에 합격하는 기쁨을 맞을 수 있기를 바라는 바이다.

2019년 1월
인터프렙어학연구소
스티븐 박

ACKNOWLEDGEMENTS

    이 책은 인터프렙의 R & D를 이끌고 있는 스티븐 박 원장님, 그리고 SAT 강의 분야에서 최고의 전문성을 가지고 감수를 맡아 주신 엄일석 부원장님, 그리고 박지현, 지치영, 임진아, 서세민, 방주희, 정지윤 선생님 등의 다년간의 강의 노하우에 기초하여 집필되었습니다.

    집필 과정에서 크고 작은 도움을 주신 인터프렙 가족들에게 진심으로 감사를 드립니다. 상담부 정재륜, 신현준 선생님, 효과적 마케팅 관련 콘셉트와 방향을 잡아 주신 강지민, 최창엽 선생님, 온라인 강의 제작과 관련하여 조언을 주신 이기욱 선생님, 멋진 표지 디자인이 나올 수 있게 도와주신 디자이너 유희정 선생님, 자료 준비 및 원고 작성 과정에서 도움을 주신 민정완, 김지원, 서희승 조교 선생님,

    그리고 SAT 수험생들이 어려워하는 부분과 필요한 내용 등에 관한 크고 작은 의견을 취합해 집필 과정에 반영하게 해 주신 강시현 부원장님과 조수민, 지효식 컨설턴트 선생님에게 진심으로 고마운 마음을 전하는 바입니다.

    또한, 출판 과정에서 교정 및 디자인 부분에서 전문적인 도움을 주신 지식과감성사의 이현 님, 나은비 님, 박솔빈 님, 안영인 님 및 그 외 스텝분들의 많은 노고에 대하여도 진심으로 감사드립니다.

2019년 1월
인터프렙 대표 정재환

Chapter 01

SAT Essay? - 그것이 알고 싶다!

- 문제 유형
- 채점 방식과 기준
- 어느 정도의 점수가 '좋은 점수'인가?

CHAPTER 01
SAT Essay? - 그것이 알고 싶다!

* SAT-Essay - 문제 유형:

Reading 파트에 나올 법한 지문을 제시한 후 그에 대한 분석을 요구하는 형태로 문제가 주어진다. 세부적으로는 지문에 대하여 "글쓴이가 'Evidence, Reasoning, Style' 적인 면에서 어떻게 자신의 주장을 효과적으로 피력하고 있는가"라는 지시 사항이 주어진다. 또한 주어진 지문을 분석하는 과정에서 수험생 자신의 의견은 제시하지 말라는 지시 사항도 같이 주어진다. 작성 시간은 50분이다. (Chapter 3부터 이러한 instruction에 충실하게 분석하고 작성하는 방법이 설명되어 있다!)

* 채점 방식과 기준:

SAT 에세이 시험은 주관식으로 두 명의 채점자가 읽기(Reading), 분석(Analysis), 쓰기(Writing) 영역별로 각각 최소 1점에서 최고 4점 시스템으로 점수를 부여한다. 두 채점자의 점수가 합산되어 각 영역별로 2점에서 8점 사이가 되고 8-8-8, 7-6-7 등의 형식으로 성적표상에 표시되며 총점은 따로 주어지지 않으나 입학 사정관들은 세 점수를 합산하여 고려하는 경우가 많다.

Reading 부분 점수는 주어진 지문의 핵심 내용과 논리의 근거 등에 대한 설명에 기초하여 어떤 주장을 어떤 근거에 의하여 하고 있다라는 점을 정확히 제시하여야 좋은 점수를 받을 수 있다.

Analysis 부분은 글쓴이가 크게 논리적 근거, 증거의 제시, 표현의 스타일 등에 관하여 어떻게 글을 작성하였는지를 자세히 설명하면 좋은 점수가 나온다.
Writing 부분은 문법, 어법에 맞게 에세이를 작성하고 단어의 선택이나 철자법 등에서 사소한 실수가 없을 경우 좋은 점수를 받을 수 있다.

적절한 작성 분량에 대한 정해진 기준은 없지만 필자와 학생들의 경험을 토대로 말하자면 일단 길어야 점수가 잘 나온다. Contents가 많을수록 분석이 깊고 또 내용에 대한 이해도 충분히 된 후 작성된 답안이라는 평가가 나오는 것이다. 답지로 주어지는 페이지의 2.5~3페이지를 채우는 것이 좋다. 단어 수로는 범위가 넓어서 대략 550~800단어 사이가 된다. (좋은 점수를 받는 경우 보통 600단어는 넘는 경우가 많고 800단어 이상인 경우도 있다. Computer-based test가 아니기 때문에 단어 수를 알 수 없지만 평소 자신의 handwriting 고려 분량을 파악하고 있어야 한다. 아무리 적어도 답지 1과 3/4페이지 또는 400단어는 작성한다는 생각으로 임할 것!)

* 어느 정도의 점수가 '좋은 점수'인가?

점수 분포를 보면 8-8-8 만점에서 7-7-7 이상을 받으면 상위 4% 이내의 '고득점'으로 간주할 수 있다. (분석 부분의 점수는 분포가 더 낮아 7-6-7 이상이어도 고득점이라고 할 수 있다.)

Collegeboard의 채점 방침에 따르면 상위 2%만 만점을 주도록 되어 있어 영역별 합계 점수에서는 8점을 받는 학생 비율이 1% 정도밖에 안된다. 분포표로 판단해 보면 상위권 대학으로 입학을 희망하는 대다수의 학생들이 분야별 점수로 5점이나 6점을 받는다고 생각할 수 있다. 그러나 SAT general score처럼 IVY League 포함 최상위권 대학으로의 진학을 희망하는 학생이라면 7-7-7 이상을 받아야 안심할 수 있다. 만약 점수가 5-5-5 또는 그 미만이라면 불이익을 받을 수 있는, 즉 심사 과정에서 '**red flag**'로 작용할 가능성이 높으므로, 더 노력하여 좀 더 높은 점수를 확보하여야 한다.

Chapter 02

SAT Essay 시험의 '성격'에 대한 이해

CHAPTER 02
SAT Essay 시험의 '성격'에 대한 이해

SAT-Essay란 무엇을 측정하기 위한 테스트인가?

It is basically a task in which you read a passage, analyze it, and explain how its argument is presented.

SAT essay는 주어진 지문을 읽고 그것을 분석한 내용을 글로써 설명하는 것이다! 여기서 특이한 점은 '주장'이 빠져 있다는 것인데, 그래서 사실 토플이나 ACT essay와는 달리 '에세이'라고 하기보다는 '설명문'에 가까운 성격을 갖는다. (아마 2016년 new SAT로 바뀌면서 이 형식을 도입하면서 Collegeboard도 이 부분에 계속 essay라는 명칭을 써야 하나라는 고민을 했을 것이다. 여러 의견이 있었을 텐데 다른 명칭을 썼을 경우 학생과 교사, 그리고 학부모 및 입학 사정관 등이 겪을 혼란을 고려하여 명칭을 유지하기로 하였을 것이다. 하긴 '에세이'의 사전적 정의가 워낙 넓어서 기술적으로 틀린 표현이 아니긴 하다.)

Points to remember:
In SAT essay, basically you read, analyze, and write about a passage.

* 왜 많은 학생들이 – 심지어 모의고사 1500대 점수가 나오는 학생들도 – SAT Essay가 어렵다고 느끼는가?

한마디로 잘 모르기 때문이다! 인간의 본성상 uncertainty는 fear로 귀결되는 경우가 많다. 지금까지 학교를 다니며 essay란 것에 막연히라도 얻은 지식에 비하여 너무 다르고 생소하다 보니 그냥 어렵다고 느끼는 것이다. 그러나 조금만 알기 시작하면 이 '편견'은 깨질 것이고 오히려 쉽다고 생각할 시점이 곧 올 것이다. 약간의 요령만 터득하면 일단 어렵게 느껴지지는 않을 텐데 이는 마치 자전거 타는 방법을 배워 본 사람들의 심정과 비유할 수 있다. 그렇게 어려워 보이던 것이 하고 나면 이제는 너무나 쉬운 것이 되어 있을 것이다.

* "Unfamiliarity breeds fear" – but don't get fearful – SAT essay task is much easier than it looks!

* 그렇지만 사실 왜 ACT-Writing-에세이 또는 심지어 TOEFL essay보다도 쉽다고 할 수 있는가?

첫째, '독해가 반'이다! 주어진 지문만 잘 이해해도 벌써 반은 점수를 딴 것이라고 할 수 있다. (이 부분은 사실 SAT 준비 과정에 있어서 효율적인 부분이기도 하다.) 독해를 연습하면 에세이가 자동적으로 준비되고 거꾸로 에세이를 준비하면서 독해력도 향상되는 것이다. (일석이조!).

둘째, '논술형' 에세이가 아니기 때문에 고심하여 자신의 주장을 생각하고 표현할 필요가 없다. 그냥 있는 그대로를 설명하면 되는 것이다. 복잡하게 주어진 지문 간의 관계나 글쓴이의 주장을 비판적으로 평가해야 하는 '논술'에 비하면 사실 '식은 죽 먹기', 말 그대로 'piece of cake'인 것이다.

* 여러 대학에서 SAT-Essay는 필수 제출 요건이 아직 아닌 경우가 많다. 그러나 누가, 또 왜 SAT-Essay 부분에 신경 써야 하는가?

일단 세부적 설명을 하기 전에, 자신이 어느 명문 대학의 입학 사정관이라고 상상을 해 보라. 그리고 심사하는 한 학생의 '스펙'에서 유독 낮은 Essay 점수가 보인다고 가정해 보라 - GPA도 좋고, SAT-General Test 점수도 1400대 후반, 그런데 Essay 점수는 3-3-4(8-8-8 만점)이다. 아무리 수상 실적이 좋고 다른 부분이 좋아도 이건 확실히 소위 불리는 **'red flag'**(입학 심사 과정에서의 결정적 결점)이다. - 입학 사정관의 기준과 해당 학교의 학풍에 따라 다르긴 해도 **대부분의 상위권 대학이라면 이 학생을 reject할 가능성이 농후**하다. (필자라면 이 학생보다는 차라리 조금 더 낮은 GPA를 가진, 그러나 괜찮은 Essay 점수(6-6-6 또는 6-5-6 정도 이상)를 가진 학생을 뽑겠다.)

기본적으로 미국 및 해외 대학 입시를 고려하는 모든 학생들이 신경 써야 한다고 할 수 있다. 왜냐하면 에세이 점수를 요구하는 학교가 상당히 많고 또 공식적으로 'required'는 아니어도 실질적으로 입학 심사 과정에서 상당히 비중 있게 고려되는 부분이기 때문이다. 일단 **UC 계열 대학에 지원하는 것을 고려하면 필수다. 일본, 홍콩, 싱가폴 등의 대학을 염두에 둘 경우**에도 그 지역 대학들 중 요구하는 경우가 있기 때문에 지원 시 선택권을 극대화하려면 일단 비교적 낮은 점수라도(예: 5-5-4 정도) 확보해 놓는 것이 좋다.

에세이 점수의 중요성은 상위권 대학일수록 더 해당된다고 할 수 있다. 왜 그럴까? 상위권(미국 랭킹 약 20위권 이상) 종합 대학 및 대부분의 비교적 소규모의 liberal arts colleges의 경우 **수업 형태를 생각하면 논리적인 답이 나온다.** 이런 대학들에서는 중하위권 대학에 비교하여 일반적으로 학점 평가 과정에서 writing의 비중

이 더 높다. 그렇기 때문에 자연스럽게 입학 사정관들이 그런 요구 사항에 잘 적응할 수 있는 학생들의 능력을 에세이 점수를 통하여 가늠하고 합-불 결정에 반영하는 것이다. 단순히 활동 이력이 많은 학생들에게 가산점을 주는 것보다 오히려 더 공정하면서도 타당한 심사 과정이라고 할 수 있다.

연세대, 고려대, 서강대 등 한국 대학이 특기자 전형이나 학생부 전형에서 해외고 졸업(또는 졸업 예정) 학생들의 서류를 심사하는 경우는 중요도가 높다고 할 수는 없지만 입학 사정관들이 new SAT 점수에 익숙해지면서 앞으로 더 비중 있게 고려할 가능성이 크다. 특히 연세대와 서강대, 성균관대 등의 경우 미국 대학과 유사한 심사 방식을 따르는 것을 수년간 느낄 수 있었는데 이러한 학교에 높은 에세이 점수를 제출할 경우 합격 가능성은 그만큼 높아질 것이다.

Chapter 03

SAT Essay
– 분석 및 작성 본격 트레이닝

1. Evidences – 기법 / 전략적 요소
2. Reasoning – 논리적 요소
3. Styles – 감성적 요소

CHAPTER 03
SAT Essay - 분석 및 작성 본격 트레이닝

여기서 잠깐!

이 Chapter의 부분별 설명을 읽기 전 우선 다음의 두 에세이 지문을 읽고 그에 대한 답을 마치 실전 시험인 것처럼 각 50분간 해 보고 계속 읽기 바란다! 이는 일종의 '소크라테스식 방식'으로 이해를 할 수 있도록 유도하기 위함인데, 일단 무언가 질문 속에서 고심하고 노력한 후 설명을 들어야 더 '깨달음'의 효과가 크기 때문이다! (이 두 지문을 예를 들어 각 파트별 설명이 있을 것이며 각각 'Apprenticeship 지문'과 'Parthenon 지문'으로 지칭할 것이다. 만약 아직 감이 안 와서 에세이를 쓰는 것이 힘들다면 적어도 지문을 읽고 내용에 대하여 대략적 이해라도 갖추고 계속 읽기 바란다.)

- ## SAT - Essay - Practice #1
  ## (for understanding the examples to be given):

  ▶ ('Apprenticeship 지문')

  > As you read the passage below, consider how Peter Downs uses
  > - evidence, such as facts or examples, to support claims.
  > - reasoning to develop ideas and to connect claims and evidence.
  > - stylistic or persuasive elements, such as word choice or appeals to emotion, to add power to the ideas expressed.

> *The passage is taken from Peter Downs, "Can't Find Skilled Workers? Start and Apprentice Program" © The Wall Street Journal. Originally published January 16, 2014.*
>
> ** Retrieved online through: https://www.wsj.com/articles/can8217t-find-skilled-workers-start-an-apprentice-program-1389917779*

1.

One key element to a competitive workforce almost entirely overlooked in the U.S. is apprenticeships. These days, American businesses typically want someone else—trade schools, community colleges, universities or even the federal government—to train their future employees. If potential future job seekers haven't been provided with the training they need, many businesses expect job seekers to take all the responsibility on themselves, often taking on serious debt without any guarantee of future employment.

2.

Worse, in the face of greater competition, many American employers are slashing training budgets and running employment software that rejects every applicant who doesn't already have the perfect combination of training and experience to perform the job on day one. Then employers lament that job applicants don't already know how to do the jobs that they want them to do. So shortsighted is this attitude that some construction companies that don't support apprenticeship programs complain that companies that do have such programs aren't training enough new workers. Yes, you read that right.

3.

This sense of entitlement contrasts sharply with attitudes in some of the world's most competitive countries, where businesses are highly involved in preparing future workers through apprenticeships. In Switzerland, 70% of young people aged 15-19 apprentice in hundreds of occupations, including baking, banking, health care, retail trade and clerical careers. In Germany, 65% of youth are in apprenticeships; in Austria 55%. All three countries have youth unemployment rates less than half of America's 16%.

4.

Last year, Greece, Italy, Latvia, Portugal, the Slovak Republic and Spain all asked Germany to help them set up similar systems. In 1997, Britain introduced a program called Modern Apprenticeships, based on the German model, and enrollment has increased every year. It now stands at 858,900. In 2012, the U.K. added apprenticeship programs for commercial pilots, lawyers, engineers and accountants that are considered the equivalent of a college education. The U.S. is headed in the opposite direction. The number of apprenticeship programs has fallen by one-third in the last decade. With only 330,578 registered apprentices in 2013, the U.S. had less than 40% of the number in Britain, a country one-fifth as populous.

5.

There are glimmers of hope that the U.S.—or at least some savvy industries—might be starting to embrace apprenticeship. In St. Louis, technology entrepreneur Jim McKelvey convinced several large employers last year—including Enterprise, Monsanto and Rawlings—that it doesn't take a college education to become good at computer programming. What it takes is working with an experienced programmer.

6.
These employers joined with Mr. McKelvey to set up what is essentially an apprenticeship program called LaunchCode. The program takes people with basic programming skills, pays them $15 an hour, and pairs them with experienced programmers for two years to give them the training to secure jobs as coders.

7.
Some employers think apprenticeships could also work in other high-tech, high-growth industries. In recent years, the U.S. Office for Apprenticeships has registered new apprenticeship programs in information technology, healthcare, biotechnology and geospatial technology.

8.
There is evidence that such apprenticeships can do more than just train young people for future careers: They can also improve students' academic performance. In the few U.S. school districts that have offered apprenticeships, high-school juniors and seniors who have been apprentices have improved in the classroom.

9.
In the Bayless School District in suburban St. Louis, for example, students who entered the district's Middle Apprenticeship Program with the Carpenters' Union had better attendance than before entering the program. The mean grade point average for these students was 1.7 at the end of their sophomore year, before they entered the apprenticeship program. By senior year, it was 3.13. They graduated with better attendance and better grades than did a group of similar students who weren't in the program.

10.
John Gaal, director of this particular apprenticeship program, credits the academic improvement to "relevance." In other words, the students saw how their classes were relevant to the careers they wanted to pursue.

11.
To the extent that the American business community is involved in education reform, they are typically investing in faddish reforms such as banning tenure, that, even if passed, would do little to ensure the competitiveness of the nation's workforce. If this same money and effort went into pushing for a two-track education system—college or apprenticeship—it would do far more to produce students prepared to compete in the 21st-century economy.

> **Instruction**
>
> *Write an essay in which you explain how Peter Downs builds the argument. In your essay, analyze how the author uses one or more of the features of evidences, reasoning, and styles (or features of your own choice) to strengthen the logic and persuasiveness of his argument. Be sure that your analysis focuses on the most relevant aspects of the passage.*
>
> *Your essay should not explain whether you agree with the author's claims, but rather explain how the author builds an argument to persuade his audience.*

• SAT - Essay - Practice #2
(for understanding the examples to be given):

▶ ('Parthenon 지문')

As you read the passage below, consider how Christopher Hitchens uses
- evidence, such as facts or examples, to support claims.
- reasoning to develop ideas and to connect claims and evidence.
- stylistic or persuasive elements, such as word choice or appeals to emotion, to add power to the ideas expressed.

The reading passage is taken from Christopher Hitchens, "The Lovely Stones." ©2009 by Condé Nast Digital. Originally published in July 2009; reprinted in Vanity Fair Magazine in July, 2009.

* *Retrieved online through*: https://www.vanityfair.com/culture/2009/07/hitchens200907

1.
The great classicist A. W. Lawrence . . . once remarked of the Parthenon that it is "the one building in the world which may be assessed as absolutely right...."

2.
Not that the beauty and symmetry of the Parthenon have not been abused and perverted and mutilated. Five centuries after the birth of Christianity the Parthenon was closed and desolated. . . . Turkish forces also used it for centuries as a garrison and an arsenal, with the tragic result that in

1687 . . . a powder magazine was detonated and huge damage inflicted on the structure. Most horrible of all, perhaps, the Acropolis was made to fly a Nazi flag during the German occupation of Athens. . . .

3.

The damage done by the ages to the building, and by past empires and occupations, cannot all be put right. But there is one desecration and dilapidation that can at least be partially undone. Early in the 19th century, Britain's ambassador to the Ottoman Empire, Lord Elgin, sent a wrecking crew to the Turkish-occupied territory of Greece, where it sawed off approximately half of the adornment of the Parthenon and carried it away. As with all things Greek, there were three elements to this, the most lavish and beautiful sculptural treasury in human history. Under the direction of the artistic genius Phidias, the temple had two massive pediments decorated with the figures of Pallas Athena, Poseidon, and the gods of the sun and the moon. It then had a series of 92 high-relief panels, or metopes, depicting a succession of mythical and historical battles. The most intricate element was the frieze, carved in bas-relief, which showed the gods, humans, and animals that made up the annual Pan-Athens procession: there were 192 equestrian warriors and auxiliaries featured, which happens to be the exact number of the city's heroes who fell at the Battle of Marathon. Experts differ on precisely what story is being told here, but the frieze was quite clearly carved as a continuous narrative. Except that half the cast of the tale is still in Bloomsbury, in London, having been sold well below cost by Elgin to the British government in 1816 for $2.2 million in today's currency to pay off his many debts. . . .

4.

. . . [T]here has been a bitter argument about the legitimacy of the British Museum's deal. I've written a whole book about this controversy and won't oppress you with all the details, but would just make this one point. If the Mona Lisa had been sawed in two during the Napoleonic Wars and the separated halves had been acquired by different museums in, say, St. Petersburg and Lisbon, would there not be a general wish to see what they might look like if re-united? If you think my analogy is overdrawn, consider this: the body of the goddess Iris is at present in London, while her head is in Athens. The front part of the torso of Poseidon is in London, and the rear part is in Athens. And so on. This is grotesque. . . .

5.
It is unfortunately true that [Athens] allowed itself to become very dirty and polluted in the 20th century, and as a result the remaining sculptures and statues on the Parthenon were nastily eroded by "acid rain." . . . But gradually and now impressively, the Greeks have been living up to their responsibilities. Beginning in 1992, the endangered marbles were removed from the temple, given careful cleaning with ultraviolet and infrared lasers, and placed in a limate-controlled interior. . . .

6.
About a thousand feet southeast of the temple [is] the astonishing new Acropolis Museum. . . . With 10 times the space of the old repository, it display[s] all the marvels that go with the temples on top of the hill. Most important, it show[s], for the first time in centuries, how the Parthenon sculptures looked to the citizens of old. . . .

7.
The British may continue in their constipated fashion to cling to what they have so crudely amputated, but . . . the Acropolis Museum has hit on the happy idea of exhibiting . . . its own original sculptures with the

London-held pieces represented by beautifully copied casts. This creates a natural thirst to see the actual re-assembly completed. So, far from emptying or weakening a museum, this controversy has created another [museum], which is destined to be among Europe's finest galleries. And one day, surely, there will be an agreement to do the right thing by the world's most "right" structure.

> **Instruction**
>
> *Write an essay in which you explain how Christopher Hitchens builds the argument. In your essay, analyze how the author uses one or more of the features of evidences, reasoning, and styles (or features of your own choice) to strengthen the logic and persuasiveness of his argument. Be sure that your analysis focuses on the most relevant aspects of the passage.*
>
> *Your essay should not explain whether you agree with the author's claims, but rather explain how the author builds an argument to persuade his audience.*

1. 전체적인 전략

지문을 받으면 약 15분간 천천히 읽으면서(총 50분) 다음의 세 부분에 대하여 지문에 있는지 확인하여 쓸 준비를 하여야 한다.

여기서 잠깐! 많은 학생들이 '그렇게나 많은 시간을 아웃라인하는 데...?'라고 반응하는 경우가 있는데 그렇게 많은 시간이 아니다. 충분히 이해하고 분석하고 또 아웃라인을 잡으려면 이 정도 또는 그 이상의 시간이 필요하다. 그리고 이 시점에서 충분히 시간을 써서 잘 계획을 세운 후 작성하면 오히려 우왕좌왕 지우고 다시 쓰고 하는 경우가 줄어 결국 시간을 절약하는 결과가 되는 경우가 대부분이다.

1. Reading 부분에 대한 준비:

일단 소개 부분을 읽으며 **어떤 사람이 어떤 주제에 대하여 누구를 주 대상으로 쓴 글**(또는 연설문)인지를 파악한다. 그리고 조금 더 심도 있게, 어떤 주장이 어떤 논리를 기반으로 제시되고 있는지를 이해하여 쓸 준비를 한다. (일부는 Analysis 부분 – Reasoning 부분에 연결되며 작성 시 일부 중복이 될 수 있으나 전혀 문제되지 않는다.)

이 Reading에 대한 평가는 학생들이 작성하는 에세이의 전체적 내용에 근거하지만, 주로 도입(Introduction) 및 결론(conclusion) 단락에서 어떻게 주장에 대한 기술을 하는지에 크게 달려 있다고 할 수 있다.

> 예1: 본 Chapter의 서두에서 주어진 연습 및 설명용 지문 첫 번째 'Apprentiship' 지문의 경우에는 다음의 밑줄 친 부분들에 초점을 두고 이해한다면(해당되지 않는 paragraphs는 이해를 위해 생략한다), 핵심 내용은 결국 "미국 기업들도 apprenticeship 제도를 숙련된 인력을 확보하는 도구로 활용해야 한다"는 주장이라는 것을 파악할 수 있다.

2.
Worse, in the face of greater competition, many American employers are slashing training budgets and running employment software that rejects every applicant who doesn't already have the perfect combination of training and experience to perform the job on day one. Then employers lament that job applicants don't already know how to do the jobs that they want them to do. So shortsighted is this attitude that some construction companies that don't support apprenticeship programs complain that companies that do have such programs aren't training enough new workers. Yes, you read that right.

3.
This sense of entitlement contrasts sharply with attitudes in some of the world's most competitive countries, where businesses are highly involved in preparing future workers through apprenticeships. In Switzerland, 70% of young people aged 15-19 apprentice in hundreds of occupations, including baking, banking, health care, retail trade and clerical careers. In Germany, 65% of youth are in apprenticeships; in Austria 55%. All three countries have youth unemployment rates less than half of America's 16%.

5.
There are glimmers of hope that the U.S.—or at least some savvy industries—might be starting to embrace apprenticeship. In St. Louis, technology entrepreneur Jim McKelvey convinced several large employers last year—including Enterprise, Monsanto and Rawlings—that it doesn't take a college education to become good at computer programming. What it takes is working with an experienced programmer.

6.

These employers joined with Mr. McKelvey to set up what is essentially an apprenticeship program called LaunchCode. The program takes people with basic programming skills, pays them $15 an hour, and pairs them with experienced programmers for two years to give them the training to secure jobs as coders.

7.

Some employers think apprenticeships could also work in other high-tech, high-growth industries. In recent years, the U.S. Office for Apprenticeships has registered new apprenticeship programs in information technology, health care, biotechnology and geospatial technology.

8.

There is evidence that such apprenticeships can do more than just train young people for future careers: They can also improve students' academic performance. In the few U.S. school districts that have offered apprenticeships, high-school juniors and seniors who have been apprentices have improved in the classroom.

11.

To the extent that the American business community is involved in education reform, they are typically investing in faddish reforms such as banning tenure, that, even if passed, would do little to ensure the competitiveness of the nation's workforce. If this same money and effort went into pushing for a two-track education system—college or apprenticeship—it would do far more to produce students prepared to compete in the 21st-century economy.

> 예2: 두 번째 연습 및 설명용 지문으로 제시되었던 'Parthenon' 지문의 예를 들면, 다음의 해당 paragraphs들의 밑줄 친 부분들에 기초하여 핵심 주장은 "Parthenon 신전의 일부 분리되어 다른 곳에 있는 박물관 등에 전시되어 있는 것을 하나로 모아 복구하는 노력이 정당한 것이다"가 되겠다.

2

Not that the beauty and symmetry of the Parthenon have not been abused and perverted and mutilated. Five centuries after the birth of Christianity the Parthenon was closed and desolated. . . . Turkish forces also used it for centuries as a garrison and an arsenal, with the tragic result that in 1687 . . . a powder magazine was detonated and huge damage inflicted on the structure. Most horrible of all, perhaps, the Acropolis was made to fly a Nazi flag during the German occupation of Athens. . . .

3

The damage done by the ages to the building, and by past empires and occupations, cannot all be put right. But there is one desecration and dilapidation that can at least be partially undone. Early in the 19th century, Britain's ambassador to the Ottoman Empire, Lord Elgin, sent a wrecking crew to the Turkish-occupied territory of Greece, where it sawed off approximately half of the adornment of the Parthenon and carried it away. As with all things Greek, there were three elements to this, the most lavish and beautiful sculptural treasury in human history. Under the direction of the artistic genius Phidias, the temple had two massive pediments decorated with the figures of Pallas Athena, Poseidon, and the gods of the sun and the moon. It then had a series of 92 high-relief panels, or metopes, depicting a succession of mythical and historical battles. The most intricate element was the frieze, carved in bas-relief, which showed the gods, humans, and animals that made up the annual Pan-Athens procession: there were 192 equestrian warriors and auxiliaries featured, which happens to be the exact number of the city's heroes who fell at the Battle of Marathon. Experts differ on precisely what story is being told here, but the frieze was quite clearly carved as a continuous narrative. Except that half the cast of the tale is still in Bloomsbury, in London, having been sold well below cost by Elgin to the British government in 1816 for $2.2 million in today's currency to pay off his many debts. . . .

4

. . . [T]here has been a bitter argument about the legitimacy of the British Museum's deal. I've written a whole book about this controversy and won't oppress you with all the details, but would just make this one point. If the Mona Lisa had been sawed in two during the Napoleonic Wars and the separated halves had been acquired by different museums in, say, St. Petersburg and Lisbon, would there not be a general wish to see what they might look like if re-united? If you think my analogy is overdrawn, consider this: the body of the goddess Iris is at present in London, while her head is in Athens. The front part of the torso of Poseidon is in London, and the rear part is in Athens. And so on. This is grotesque. . . .

7

The British may continue in their constipated fashion to cling to what they have so crudely amputated, but . . . the Acropolis Museum has hit on the happy idea of exhibiting . . . its own original sculptures with the London-held pieces represented by beautifully copied casts. This creates a natural thirst to see the actual re-assembly completed. So, far from emptying or weakening a museum, this controversy has created another [museum], which is destined to be among Europe's finest galleries. And one day, surely, there will be an agreement to do the right thing by the world's most "right" structure.

 작성 트레이닝:

이렇게 이해한 'Apprenticeship' - Reading 관련 내용은 주로 Introduction 및 conclusion 단락에서 작성 시 반영하면 되는데 그 예는 다음과 같다:

> **Introduction**
> Peter Downs writes "Can't find Skilled Workers? Start an Apprentice Program" in an attempt to persuade the readers that businesses in the U.S. should take advantage of apprenticeships in their employment practices. Throughout the passage, Downs projects a strong message about implementing apprenticeships by using statistical data, concrete cases, cause-effect reasoning, and contrasts. These strategic, reasoning, and stylistic elements in his article buttress the persuasiveness of his argument to the readers about the merits of apprenticeship.

> **Conclusion**
> The author effectively used exact data, concrete cases, consequential and cause-effect reasoning, and contrasts his essay. Together, these strategies resulted in successfully persuading the readers that the practice of apprenticeship should be much more frequently and eagerly implemented by businesses in the U.S.

이어서 'Parthenon' 지문에 대한 Reading 관련을 Introduction 및 conclusion 단락에서 작성해 보면 다음과 같다.

Introduction
Christopher Hitchens writes "The Lovely Stones" in an attempt to persuade the audience that the original sculptures from the Parthenon must be returned to Greece. Throughout the passage, Hitchens projects a strong message about the sculptures' relocation through, historical and statistical data, moral reasoning, contrasts, and analogies. These elements and strategies buttress the persuasiveness of his argument to the readers.

Conclusion
Hitchens's argument is elaborately and skillfully constructed with exact data, moral reasoning, contrast, and allusion. By utilizing these components in his argument, the author successfully delivered a clear and convincing message to the readers regarding the righteousness of returning the original Parthenon sculptures to Greece.

트레이너 Tip:

- 이 부분에 대하여 좋은 평가를 받는 답안은 단순히 "내용 자체가 무엇인가" 또는 "논리가 어떻다"라고 기술하는 것보다는 그 둘을 결합시켜 "이러한 논리로 이러이러한 주장을 하고 있다"라고 전체적인 이해를 나타내는 방식으로 써야 한다! 이렇게 융합적으로 전체적인 내용을 염두에 두고 기술하면 "이 학생이 제대로 지문을 읽고 (그래서 'Reading 점수') 이해했구나…"라는 느낌을 체점자에게 확실히 전달할 수 있는 것이다.

- 작성 시 글쓴이가 주어인 동사의 시제는 현재형으로 통일하는 것이 좋다. 사실 이미 작성된 것이고 주장된 것이기 때문에 과거형으로 쓰는 것이 더 맞다고 느껴질 수 있으나 분석글이나 기사문의 특성을 고려하여 '현장감' 있게 현재형 동사로 기술하는 것이 적당하다. (그러나 일관성 있게 모두 과거형으로 기술해도 전혀 문제될 것은 없으니 평소 연습할 때 한 방향을 결정하여 습관화시켜 둘 것!)

효과적 Reading을 위한 추가적 트레이너 Tip:

- 전체적인 내용을 파악하는 것은 쉽지 않다. 일단 "나무를 보는 것이 아니라 숲을 보겠다"라는 마음 자세로, 또한 반드시 앞부분에서 나온 내용이 글 말미까지 유지된다는 보장이 없다는 유연한 마음가짐으로 부단히 연습하여서 글쓴이의 의도를 파악하는 reading 능력을 갖추어야 한다.

- 이 '유연함' 속에는 일부분을 무시하고 이해를 시도하는 리딩 전략도 포함된다. 예를 들어 저자의 주장이 "the minimum wage increases should continue"라면 중간에 "the unusually rapid speed at which the rate has been increasing is hurting the economy"라고 나오는 부분은 어느 정도 무시하고 흐름을 이어가며 이해를 해야 혼란스럽지 않고 효율적인 독해를 할 수 있는 것이다.

- 지문의 출처를 밝히는 시작 부분에 제시되는 글의 '제목' 자체가 이해를 돕는 경우가 많으니 신경 써서 볼 것이며, 앞부분보다는 끝부분에 결정적으로 주장의 핵심이 다시 정리되어 제시되는 경우가 많음을 기억하면 효과적으로 접근하는 데 도움이 될 것이다.

- SAT Reading 부분에 대하여 문제를 풀고 이해를 한 후 다시 복습 시 그냥 지문만을 여러 번 읽는 것도 리딩 감각을 향상시키는 데 도움이 된다. Essay 작성을 해야 된다는 생각으로 분석적인 요소들이 어떻게 되는지 파악하면서 읽는 습관을 들이자!

- 항상 어휘는 모르는 것이 나오면 일단 앞뒤 문맥에 'series cue'가 있는지 확인해서 이해하는 습관적 노력을 하라 - 예를 들어 'ubiquitous'라는 단어가 나온 후 'it is seen just about everywhere'라는 표현이 잠시 후 따라온다든가, 'indisyncracy'라는 표현 이전에 'individual peculiarity'라는 언급이 있었으면 그들을 하나의 'series'로 묶어서 같은 뜻으로 이해할 수 있는 것이다. 이렇게 하면 모르는 단어 때문에 이해의 흐름이 끊기거나 공부하는 데 있어 frustration을 피하는 데 도움이 된다.

2. Analysis 부분에 대한 준비:

본격적인 본문 부분에 해당되는 내용을 분석하여 쓸 준비를 하는 부분이다. Introduction에 나온 똑같은 순서대로 분석하고 기술하는 것이 좋다: evidences, reasoning, styles.

A. Evidences – 기법 / 전략적 요소:

말 그대로 하면 '증거 제시'가 되지만 의미를 생각하면 '어떤 방식'으로 지문의 주장이 설득력 있게 제시되고 있는가에 대한 분석이다. 예를 들면 교육부에서 발표한 통계에 근거하거나 또는 어떤 학자가 발표한 이론에 근거하여 글쓴이의 주장의 근거를 제시하는 경우가 해당된다.

이 요소에 대하여 지문을 분석하였을 때 주로 발견할 수 있는 요소들은 다음과 같다.

1. **Use of statistics / data**: 각종 통계적 사실을 인용하는 경우 – 지문에 숫자가 있는 부분만을 살펴도 비교적 쉽게 확인이 되는 내용이다.

> 예1: 서두에서 주어진 첫 번째 문제 'Apprenticeship' 지문의 경우에는 다음의 밑줄 친 부분들이 해당된다.

3.
This sense of entitlement contrasts sharply with attitudes in some of the world's most competitive countries, where businesses are highly involved in preparing future workers through apprenticeships. In Switzerland, 70% of young people aged 15-19 apprentice in hundreds of occupations, including baking, banking, health care, retail trade and clerical careers. In Germany, 65% of youth are in apprenticeships; in Austria 55%. All three countries have youth unemployment rates less than half of America's 16%.

4.
Last year, Greece, Italy, Latvia, Portugal, the Slovak Republic and Spain all asked Germany to help them set up similar systems. In 1997, Britain introduced a program called Modern Apprenticeships, based on the German model, and enrollment has increased every year. It now stands at 858,900. In 2012, the U.K. added apprenticeship programs for commercial pilots, lawyers, engineers and accountants that are considered the equivalent of a college education. The U.S. is headed in the opposite direction. The number of apprenticeship programs has fallen by one-third in the last decade. With only 330,578 registered apprentices in 2013, the U.S. had less than 40% of the number in Britain, a country one-fifth as populous.

9.
In the Bayless School District in suburban St. Louis, for example, students who entered the district's Middle Apprenticeship Program with the Carpenters' Union had better attendance than before entering the program. The mean grade point average for these students was 1.7 at the end of their sophomore year, before they entered the apprenticeship program. By senior year, it was 3.13. They graduated with better attendance and better grades than did a group of similar students who weren't in the program.

> 예2: 서두에서 주어진 두 번째 문제 'Parthenon' 지문의 경우에는 다음의 밑줄 친 부분들이 해당된다.

3

The damage done by the ages to the building, and by past empires and occupations, cannot all be put right. But there is one desecration and dilapidation that can at least be partially undone. Early in the 19th century, Britain's ambassador to the Ottoman Empire, Lord Elgin, sent a wrecking crew to the Turkish-occupied territory of Greece, where it sawed off approximately half of the adornment of the Parthenon and carried it away. As with all things Greek, there were three elements to this, the most lavish and beautiful sculptural treasury in human history. Under the direction of the artistic genius Phidias, the temple had two massive pediments decorated with the figures of Pallas Athena, Poseidon, and the gods of the sun and the moon. <u>It then had a series of 92 high-relief panels, or metopes, depicting a succession of mythical and historical battles. The most intricate element was the frieze, carved in bas-relief, which showed the gods, humans, and animals that made up the annual Pan-Athens procession: there were 192 equestrian warriors and auxiliaries featured, which happens to be the exact number of the city's heroes who fell at the Battle of Marathon. Experts differ on precisely what story is being told here, but the frieze was quite clearly carved as a continuous narrative. Except that half the cast of the tale is still in Bloomsbury, in London, having been sold well below cost by Elgin to the British government in 1816 for $2.2 million in today's currency to pay off his many debts.</u> . . .

6

About a thousand feet southeast of the temple [is] the astonishing new Acropolis Museum. . . . With 10 times the space of the old repository, it display[s] all the marvels that go with the temples on top of the hill. Most important, it show[s], for the first time in centuries, how the Parthenon sculptures looked to the citizens of old. . . .

2. Citing case studies / mentioning research findings:
잘 알려진 또는 학술적으로 연구된 사례를 인용하는 경우 – 집합적 수치보다는 정확한 경우를 증거로 제시하여 설득력을 높이는 기법이다.

> 예1: 'Apprenticeship' 지문의 경우는 다음의 밑줄 친 부분이 이에 해당된다.

5.

There are glimmers of hope that the U.S.—or at least some savvy industries—might be starting to embrace apprenticeship. In St. Louis, technology entrepreneur Jim McKelvey convinced several large employers last year—including Enterprise, Monsanto and Rawlings—that it doesn't take a college education to become good at computer programming. What it takes is working with an experienced programmer.

6.

These employers joined with Mr. McKelvey to set up what is essentially an apprenticeship program called LaunchCode. The program takes people with basic programming skills, pays them $15 an hour, and pairs them with experienced programmers for two years to give them the training to secure jobs as coders.

9.

In the Bayless School District in suburban St. Louis, for example, students who entered the district's Middle Apprenticeship Program with the Carpenters' Union had better attendance than before entering the program. The mean grade point average for these students was 1.7 at the end of their sophomore year, before they entered the apprenticeship program. By senior year, it was 3.13. They graduated with better attendance and better grades than did a group of similar students who weren't in the program.

> 예2: 'Parthenon' 지문의 경우는 다음의 밑줄 친 부분이 이에 해당된다.

2

Not that the beauty and symmetry of the Parthenon have not been abused and perverted and mutilated. Five centuries after the birth of Christianity the Parthenon was closed and desolated. . . . Turkish forces also used it for centuries as a garrison and an arsenal, with the tragic result that in 1687 . . . a powder magazine was detonated and huge damage inflicted on the structure. Most horrible of all, perhaps, the Acropolis was made to fly a Nazi flag during the German occupation of Athens. . . .

3

The damage done by the ages to the building, and by past empires and occupations, cannot all be put right. But there is one desecration and dilapidation that can at least be partially undone. <u>Early in the 19th century, Britain's ambassador to the Ottoman Empire, Lord Elgin, sent a wrecking crew to the Turkish-occupied territory of Greece, where it sawed off approximately half of the adornment of the Parthenon and carried it away.</u> As with all things Greek, there were three elements to this, the most lavish and beautiful sculptural treasury in human history. Under the direction of the artistic genius Phidias, the temple had two massive pediments decorated with the figures of Pallas Athena, Poseidon, and the gods of the sun and the moon. It then had a series of 92 high-relief panels, or metopes, depicting a succession of mythical and historical battles. The most intricate element was the frieze, carved in bas-relief, which showed the gods, humans, and animals that made up the annual Pan-Athens procession: there were 192 equestrian warriors and auxiliaries featured, which happens to be the exact number of the city's heroes who fell at the Battle of Marathon. Experts differ on precisely what story is being told here, but the frieze was quite clearly carved as a continuous narrative. Except that half the cast of the tale is still in Bloomsbury, in London, having been sold well below cost by Elgin to the British government in 1816 for $2.2 million in today's currency to pay off his many debts. . . .

5

It is unfortunately true that [Athens] allowed itself to become very dirty and polluted in the 20th century, and as a result the remaining sculptures and statues on the Parthenon were nastily eroded by "acid rain." . . . But gradually and now impressively, the Greeks have been living up to their responsibilities. Beginning in 1992, the endangered marbles were removed from the temple, given careful cleaning with ultraviolet and infrared lasers, and placed in a limate-controlled interior. . . .

6

About a thousand feet southeast of the temple [is] the astonishing new Acropolis Museum. . . . With 10 times the space of the old repository, it display[s] all the marvels that go with the temples on top of the hill. Most important, it show[s], for the first time in centuries, how the Parthenon sculptures looked to the citizens of old. . . .

3. Reference to authorities: 주어진 분야에서 권위가 있는 전문가나 기관, 또는 일반적으로 잘 알려진 지도자의 주장이나 발언 내용 등을 언급하며 argument에 힘을 싣는 경우이다.

> 예1: 'Apprenticeship' 지문의 경우는 다음의 밑줄 친 부분이 이에 해당된다.
> (Case studies와 일부 중복될 수 있으나 문제없다.)

5.

There are glimmers of hope that the U.S.—or at least some savvy industries—might be starting to embrace apprenticeship. In St. Louis, technology entrepreneur Jim McKelvey convinced several large employers last year—including Enterprise, Monsanto and Rawlings—that it doesn't take a college education to become good at computer programming. What it takes is working with an experienced programmer.

10.
John Gaal, director of this particular apprenticeship program, credits the academic improvement to "relevance." In other words, the students saw how their classes were relevant to the careers they wanted to pursue.

> 예2: 'Parthenon' 지문의 경우는 다음의 밑줄 친 부분 하나만 이에 해당된다.

1
The great classicist A. W. Lawrence . . . once remarked of the Parthenon that it is "the one building in the world which may be assessed as absolutely right." . . .

작성 트레이닝:

이러한 분석을 기반으로 하여 답안의 본론 부분의 첫 paragraph – evidence 관련 단락을 작성해 보면 다음과 같다.

우선 Apprenticeship의 경우:

Regarding the strategies, Downs's first approach is the use of statistical data. He refers to numerous statistics throughout his essay regarding the benefits of apprenticeships for businesses. In paragraph 3, he points out that "In Switzerland, 70% of young people aged 15-19 apprentice in hundreds of occupations… In Germany, 65% of youth…; in Austria 55%. All three countries have youth unemployment rates less than half of America's 16%." Then, in the 4th paragraph, he presents the data about the differences between the U.S. and England by describing that "With only 330,578 registered apprentices…, the U.S. had less than 40% of the number in Britain…" Later in the essay, he presents the differences between the high-school students who go through apprenticeship and those who don't; "The mean grade point average for these students was 1.7 at the end of their sophomore year… By senior year, it was 3.13." *Then, the author also cites actual cases to further strengthen the trustworthiness, and thus the logical quality of his argument.* Downs introduces the case of an entrepreneur Jim McKelvey who successfully induced companies like 'Enterprise, Monsanto and Rawlings'… as a way to back up the benefits of apprenticeship. He elaborates on the program that these enterprises established, called 'LanuchCode,' which takes in people with just basic programming skills and trains them to be coders… Downs further cites the fact that "the U.S. Office for Apprenticeships has registered new apprenticeship programs in information technology, health care, [etc.]" Then, in paragraph 9, the positive impacts of apprenticeship programs on the academic performances of young students in the "Bayless School District in suburban St. Louis' were referred to as a specific case. These statistical data and references to actual cases boost the credibility of the author's message.

그리고 Parthenon의 경우 다음처럼 작성할 수 있다:

When the evidences in the article are examined, the author's strategy in presenting argument is making references to exact historical and current data to beef up the logical quality of his argument. He first describes Parthenon with highly detailed references to its features like, "92 high-relief panels," "192 equestrian warriors and auxiliaries," etc. Then he points to the injustice by describing the fact that the precious pieces of the structure were "sold well below cost by Elgin to the British government in 1816 for $2.2 million in today's currency" which is a small amount for a great historical treasure. He also mentions how the Greeks saved the remaining sculptures and statues and are preserving their beauty in a museum away from the dangerous effects of the elements, "[w]ith 10 times the space of the old repository, it display[s] all the marvels that go with the temples on top of the hill..." His descriptions of how Greeks are treating the sculptures right "with ultraviolet and infra-red lasers..." offer realistic pictures about what should be done. Together, these detailed and factual references strengthen the logical appeal of his message.

트레이너 Tip:

- 출제되는 지문의 대략 80% 정도나 되는 많은 경우에 statistics / data는 포함하기 때문에 일단 이 부분은 지문을 비교적 빠르게 스캔하면서 찾아서 기술하겠다는 마음가짐으로 임하면 효율을 높일 수 있다.

- 먼저 statistics / data로 제시된 부분의 일부가 다시 specific case(s)로 제시될 수도 있으나 초점이 달라 중복이라고 볼 수 없으므로 당황하지 말고 전부 포함시키면 된다.

- References to authority와 관련하여서는 authority가 있는 사람이나 기관이 나왔다 하여도 글의 목적과 흐름으로 보아서는 전문성이나 대표성의 이유가 아닌 경우도 있으니 주의해야 한다. (때로는 authority figure나 organization이 counter-argument의 소스이거나, 예외 또는 나쁜 예로 인용되는 경우도 있을 수 있다는 것을 염두에 둘 것.)

B. Reasoning - 논리적 요소:

글쓴이가 어떤 **논거, 즉 주장의 근거를 어떻게 설명**하면서 글을 읽거나 연설을 듣는 사람들을 설득하고 있는지를 설명하여야 하는 부분이다. 예를 들면 미세먼지 감소 대책에서 가장 시급한 것은 지금 당장 화력발전소 가동 중단인데 그 이유는 석탄을 연료로 하는 화력발전소가 가장 큰 미세먼지 유발 요인(원인)이기 때문이다라고 주장한다면 이는 "원인-결과의 분석(cause and effect analysis)에 기초한 논거"를 제시하는 경우라고 할 수 있는 것이다.

(Reasoning의 유형에 대하여 '논술적' 마인드가 부족하다고 느낀다면 Appendix B - "Reasoning Patterns - logical rules of thinking"에서 정리된 내용을 참고하기 바란다.)

이 부분에 관하여 분석하면 주로 발견할 수 있는 요소들은 다음과 같다.

1. Explaining the cause-effect relationships + pointing to the positive / negative consequences: '인과관계' 또는 예상되는 긍정적/부정적 결과를 설명하여 주장의 논거로 제시하는 경우.

> 예1: 'Apprenticeship' 지문의 경우는 다음의 밑줄 친 부분이 이에 해당되는데 주로 'positive, beneficial consequences'에 관한 내용이다.

3.
This sense of entitlement contrasts sharply with attitudes in some of the world's most competitive countries, where businesses are highly involved

in preparing future workers through apprenticeships. In Switzerland, 70% of young people aged 15-19 apprentice in hundreds of occupations, including baking, banking, health care, retail trade and clerical careers. In Germany, 65% of youth are in apprenticeships; in Austria 55%. All three countries have youth unemployment rates less than half of America's 16%.

4.

Last year, Greece, Italy, Latvia, Portugal, the Slovak Republic and Spain all asked Germany to help them set up similar systems. In 1997, Britain introduced a program called Modern Apprenticeships, based on the German model, and enrollment has increased every year. It now stands at 858,900. In 2012, the U.K. added apprenticeship programs for commercial pilots, lawyers, engineers and accountants that are considered the equivalent of a college education. The U.S. is headed in the opposite direction. The number of apprenticeship programs has fallen by one-third in the last decade. With only 330,578 registered apprentices in 2013, the U.S. had less than 40% of the number in Britain, a country one-fifth as populous.

8.

There is evidence that such apprenticeships can do more than just train young people for future careers: They can also improve students' academic performance. In the few U.S. school districts that have offered apprenticeships, high-school juniors and seniors who have been apprentices have improved in the classroom.

10.

John Gaal, director of this particular apprenticeship program, credits the academic improvement to "relevance." In other words, the students saw how their classes were relevant to the careers they wanted to pursue.

11.

To the extent that the American business community is involved in education reform, they are typically investing in faddish reforms such as banning tenure, that, even if passed, would do little to ensure the competitiveness of the nation's workforce. If this same money and effort went into pushing for a two-track education system—college or apprenticeship—it would do far more to produce students prepared to compete in the 21st-century economy.

> 예2: (이 부분에 관련하여 'Parthenon' 지문의 경우에는 글쓴이가 주로 'Moral reasoning'에 의존하고 있기 때문에 해당 사항이 없다.)

2. Recognizing counter-arguments, but pointing out the logical flaws in them: 반대 의견이 있음을 인정하지만 그것의 논리적 문제점을 지적하여 글쓴이의 주장의 근거로 제시하는 경우(+ 상대 입장의 극단성을 지적하는 경우도 포함).

> 예1: 'Apprenticeship' 지문의 경우 main reasoning approach는 아니지만 다음의 밑줄 친 부분이 이에 해당된다.

1.

One key element to a competitive workforce almost entirely overlooked in the U.S. is apprenticeships. These days, American businesses typically want someone else—trade schools, community colleges, universities or even the federal government—to train their future employees. If potential future job seekers haven't been provided with the training they need, many businesses expect job seekers to take all the responsibility on themselves, often taking on serious debt without any guarantee of future employment.

2.

Worse, in the face of greater competition, many American employers are slashing training budgets and running employment software that rejects every applicant who doesn't already have the perfect combination of training and experience to perform the job on day one. Then employers lament that job applicants don't already know how to do the jobs that they want them to do. So shortsighted is this attitude that some construction companies that don't support apprenticeship programs complain that companies that do have such programs aren't training enough new workers. Yes, you read that right.

11.

To the extent that the American business community is involved in education reform, they are typically investing in faddish reforms such as banning tenure, that, even if passed, would do little to ensure the competitiveness of the nation's workforce. If this same money and effort went into pushing for a two-track education system—college or apprenticeship—it would do far more to produce students prepared to compete in the 21st-century economy.

> 예2: 'Parthenon' 지문 역시 이러한 reasoning이 주 논리는 아니기 때문에 다음의 한 부분에서만 이 사항이 어느 정도만 포함되어 있다고 할 수 있다. (반대 의견이라기보다는 절충안이 시도되고 그것이 결국 오히려 글쓴이의 주장을 더 강화하는 결과를 가져온다는 논리가 담겨 있다.)

7.
The British may continue in their constipated fashion to cling to what they have so crudely amputated, but . . . <u>the Acropolis Museum has hit on the happy idea of exhibiting . . . its own original sculptures with the London-held pieces represented by beautifully copied casts.</u> This creates a natural thirst to see the actual re-assembly completed. So, far from emptying or weakening a museum, this controversy has created another [museum], which is destined to be among Europe's finest galleries. And one day, surely, there will be an agreement to do the right thing by the world's most "right" structure.

3. Moral / ethical reasoning based on the widely accepted norms or basic principles of well-established social systems such as democracy and capitalism.

<u>주장이 나오게 된 역사적 배경이나 사회의 도덕적 또는 윤리적 가치관, 또는 민주주의, 자본주의의 원칙 등을 설명하면서 그 주장의 당위성이나 필연성 등을 연결시키는 경우.</u>

> 예1: ('Apprenticeship' 지문의 경우에는 이에 해당하는 reasoning은 언급된 바가 없다.)

> 예2: 'Parthenon' 지문에서는 글 전체에 고르게 나타나 있는데 다음의 밑줄 친 부분이 특히 이에 해당된다고 할 수 있다.

1.

The great classicist A. W. Lawrence . . . once remarked of the Parthenon that it is "the one building in the world which may be assessed as absolutely right.". . .

2.

Not that the beauty and symmetry of the Parthenon have not been abused and perverted and mutilated. Five centuries after the birth of Christianity the Parthenon was closed and desolated. . . . Turkish forces also used it for centuries as a garrison and an arsenal, with the tragic result that in 1687 . . . a powder magazine was detonated and huge damage inflicted on the structure. Most horrible of all, perhaps, the Acropolis was made to fly a Nazi flag during the German occupation of Athens. . . .

3.

The damage done by the ages to the building, and by past empires and occupations, cannot all be put right. But there is one desecration and dilapidation that can at least be partially undone. Early in the 19th century,

Britain's ambassador to the Ottoman Empire, Lord Elgin, sent a wrecking crew to the Turkish-occupied territory of Greece, where it sawed off approximately half of the adornment of the Parthenon and carried it away. As with all things Greek, there were three elements to this, the most lavish and beautiful sculptural treasury in human history. Under the direction of the artistic genius Phidias, the temple had two massive pediments decorated with the figures of Pallas Athena, Poseidon, and the gods of the sun and the moon. It then had a series of 92 high-relief panels, or metopes, depicting a succession of mythical and historical battles. The most intricate element was the frieze, carved in bas-relief, which showed the gods, humans, and animals that made up the annual Pan-Athens procession: there were 192 equestrian warriors and auxiliaries featured, which happens to be the exact number of the city's heroes who fell at the Battle of Marathon. Experts differ on precisely what story is being told here, but the frieze was quite clearly carved as a continuous narrative. Except that half the cast of the tale is still in Bloomsbury, in London, having been sold well below cost by Elgin to the British government in 1816 for $2.2 million in today's currency to pay off his many debts. . . .

4.

. . . [T]here has been a bitter argument about the legitimacy of the British Museum's deal. I've written a whole book about this controversy and won't oppress you with all the details, but would just make this one point. If the Mona Lisa had been sawed in two during the Napoleonic Wars and the separated halves had been acquired by different museums in, say, St. Petersburg and Lisbon, would there not be a general wish to see what they might look like if re-united? If you think my analogy is overdrawn, consider this: the body of the goddess Iris is at present in London, while her head is in Athens. The front part of the torso of Poseidon is in London, and the rear part is in Athens. And so on. This is grotesque. . . .

7.
The British may continue in their constipated fashion to cling to what they have so crudely amputated, but . . . the Acropolis Museum has hit on the happy idea of exhibiting . . . its own original sculptures with the London-held pieces represented by beautifully copied casts. This creates a natural thirst to see the actual re-assembly completed. So, far from emptying or weakening a museum, this controversy has created another [museum], which is destined to be among Europe's finest galleries. And one day, surely, there will be an <u>agreement to do the right thing by the world's most "right" structure</u>.

 작성 트레이닝:

이러한 분석을 기반으로 하여 답안의 본론 부분의 둘째 paragraph – reasoning 관련 단락을 작성해 보면 다음과 같다.

우선 'Apprenticeship'의 경우 다음과 같은 작성이 가능하다:

> **Next, in terms of the reasoning involved,** <u>the author basically offers the consequential reasoning regarding the benefits of apprenticeship programs, and how they can be the solution for some U.S. businesses that cannot find enough skilled workers.</u>

> *In the 3rd paragraph, when he describes that differences between the U.S. and the European countries regarding the use of apprenticeships, the reasoning is that the U.S. businesses should also reap the benefits by following the Europeans. Also, in paragraph 4, when he cites the actual cases, his logic is essentially that those programs bring huge benefits for the companies that use apprenticeship programs. Then, Downs also turned to the cause-effect reasoning when he explained the effects of the program on the students who go through the apprenticeships; he offers elaborate explanations on how being in the program 'causes' the students to see the connection between what they learn and what they may be doing in their future jobs, resulting in the 'effects' of motivating them and boosting their attendance records and GPAs. Together, these reasoning elements buttress the logical appeal of his message.*

그리고 'Parthenon'의 경우는 다음이 적절한 작성의 예이다:

> *<u>Then, when the reasoning aspect is scrutinized, the author relied mostly on the moral reasoning. Hitchens used the word 'right' several times throughout his essay, which is the indication that he is mostly relying on reminding people of what is the morally desirable action to be taken regarding the issue.</u> Right from the beginning in paragraph 1, he quotes the great classicist A. W. Lawrence's statement "the one building in the world which may be assessed as absolutely right." In the last paragraph, the author describes the consensus among nations involved regarding the return of the sculptures to Greece as "agreement to do the right thing by the world's most "right" structure." Then, he describes what have been "done by past empires and occupations..." as "desecration and dilapidation", indicating that they were wrong and thus must be "undone" by returning the pieces to Greece. These reasoning aspects also buttress the persuasiveness of his argument.*

트레이너 Tip:

- 경우에 따라 딱히 Reasoning에서 특성 있는 frame이 느껴지지 않는 경우가 있는데 그래도 잘 분석하여 보면 나오는 경우가 많다. 또한 상식적으로 생각하여 어떤 '틀'에 해당되지 않더라도 글쓴이의 의도에 대하여 자연스럽게 기술하여도 점수를 인정받을 수 있다. (예: "겉으로 드러나는 부분이 아닌 세부적 분석을 통해 일반인들이 느끼는 사항이 잘못된 인식이라는 논리를 펴고 있다." 이렇게 기술하여도 타당할 수 있는 것이다.)

- 여기서 명시된 사항보다 조금 더 자세히 reasoning frameworks에 대하여 준비할 수 있도록 Appendix B 부분 – "Reasoning Pattern / Logical Thinking에 대한 정리"에서 기술하여 놓았으니 고득점(또는 만점!)을 필히 취득하고자 한다면 참고하기 바란다.

C. Stylistic elements - 스타일적인 요소

이 부분은 내용이나 논리와 분리되어 **글의 감성적 요소를 분석하는 파트이다.** 예를 들면 1인칭 관점(first person perspective)의 언어 사용으로 글쓴이의 개인적 애착이나 집념 등을 전달하는 스타일이 있을 수 있고, 또는 과장법(hyperbole)을 사용하여 글이나 연설의 감성적 호소력을 높이는 경우가 있을 수 있다.

이 요소와 관련하여 분석하였을 때 주로 발견할 수 있는 요소들은 다음과 같다.

1. Personal anecdotes + first person language / perspectives: 개인적 일화 소개 및 1인칭 관점의 언어 사용을 통한 호소력 재고.

> 예: 'Apprenticeship' 및 'Parthenon' 지문에서는 이 스타일적 요소는 쓰이지 않았고, Martin Luther King, Jr. 목사의 연설문 중 다음의 밑줄 친 부분에서 반복적으로 'I'와 'We'가 쓰인 것을 보면 이 방식이 어떻게 글에서 사용되어 호소력을 높일 수 있는지 알 수 있다.

1.

Since I am a preacher by calling, I suppose it is not surprising that I have . . . major reasons for bringing Vietnam into the field of my moral vision. There is at the outset a very obvious and almost facile connection between the war in Vietnam and the struggle I, and others, have been waging in America. A few years ago there was a shining moment in that struggle. It seemed as if there was a real promise of hope for the poor—both black and white—through the poverty program. There were experiments, hopes, new beginnings. Then came the buildup in Vietnam, and I watched this program broken and eviscerated, as if it were some idle political plaything of a society gone mad on war, and I knew that America would never invest the necessary funds or energies in rehabilitation of its poor so long as adventures like Vietnam continued to draw men and skills and money like some demonic destructive suction tube. So, I was increasingly compelled to see the war as an enemy of the poor and to attack it as such.

2.

Perhaps a more tragic recognition of reality took place when it became clear to me that the war was doing far more than devastating the hopes of the poor at home. It was sending their sons and their brothers and their husbands to fight and to die in extraordinarily high proportions relative to the rest of the population. We were taking the black young men who had been crippled by our society and sending them eight thousand miles away to guarantee liberties in Southeast Asia which they had not found in southwest Georgia and East Harlem. And so we have been repeatedly faced with the cruel irony of watching Negro and white boys on TV screens as they kill and die together for a nation that has been unable to seat them together in the same schools. And so we watch them in brutal solidarity burning the huts of a poor village, but we realize that they would hardly live on the same block in Chicago. I could not be silent in the face of such cruel manipulation of the poor.

2. Contrasts / parallelism (juxtaposition) / repetitions: 대조, 병치, 반복 등을 통하여 강조 효과를 높이는 스타일적 요소.

> 예1: 'Apprenticeship' 지문의 경우는 다음 밑줄 친 부분이 해당된다.

1.

One key element to a competitive workforce almost **entirely overlooked** in the U.S. is apprenticeships. These days, American businesses typically want someone else—trade schools, community colleges, universities or even the federal government—to train their future employees. If potential future job seekers haven't been provided with the training they need, many businesses expect job seekers to take all the responsibility on themselves, often taking on serious debt without any guarantee of future employment.

3.

This sense of entitlement contrasts sharply with attitudes in some of the world's most competitive countries, where businesses are **highly involved** in preparing future workers through apprenticeships. In Switzerland, 70% of young people aged 15-19 apprentice in hundreds of occupations, including baking, banking, health care, retail trade and clerical careers. In Germany, 65% of youth are in apprenticeships; in Austria 55%. All three countries have youth unemployment rates less than half of America's 16%.

4.

Last year, Greece, Italy, Latvia, Portugal, the Slovak Republic and Spain all asked Germany to help them set up similar systems. In 1997, Britain introduced a program called Modern Apprenticeships, based on the German model, and enrollment has increased every year. It now stands at 858,900. In 2012, the U.K. added apprenticeship programs for commercial pilots, lawyers, engineers and accountants that are considered the equivalent of a college education. The U.S. is headed in the opposite direction. The number of apprenticeship programs has fallen by one-third in the last decade. With only 330,578 registered apprentices in 2013, the U.S. had less than 40% of the number in Britain, a country one-fifth as populous.

> 예2: 'Parthenon' 지문에서는 다음의 밑줄 친 부분이다.

1.

The great classicist A. W. Lawrence . . . once remarked of the Parthenon that it is "the one building in the world which may be assessed as absolutely **right**." . . .

2.

Not that the beauty and symmetry of the Parthenon have not been abused and perverted and mutilated. Five centuries after the birth of Christianity the Parthenon was closed and desolated. . . . Turkish forces also used it for centuries as a garrison and an arsenal, with the tragic result that in 1687 . . . a powder magazine was detonated and huge damage inflicted on the structure. Most horrible of all, perhaps, the Acropolis was made to fly a Nazi flag during the German occupation of Athens. . . .

3.
The damage done by the ages to the building, and by past empires and occupations, can**not** all be put **right**. But there is one desecration and dilapidation that can at least be partially undone. Early in the 19th century, Britain's ambassador to the Ottoman Empire, Lord Elgin, sent a wrecking crew to the Turkish-occupied territory of Greece, where it sawed off approximately half of the adornment of the Parthenon and carried it away. As with all things Greek, there were three elements to this, the most lavish and beautiful sculptural treasury in human history. Under the direction of the artistic genius Phidias, the temple had two massive pediments decorated with the figures of Pallas Athena, Poseidon, and the gods of the sun and the moon. It then had a series of 92 high-relief panels, or metopes, depicting a succession of mythical and historical battles. The most intricate element was the frieze, carved in bas-relief, which showed the gods, humans, and animals that made up the annual Pan-Athens procession: there were 192 equestrian warriors and auxiliaries featured, which happens to be the exact number of the city's heroes who fell at the Battle of Marathon. Experts differ on precisely what story is being told here, but the frieze was quite clearly carved as a continuous narrative. Except that half the cast of the tale is still in Bloomsbury, in London, having been sold well below cost by Elgin to the British government in 1816 for $2.2 million in today's currency to pay off his many debts. . . .

7.
The British may continue in their constipated fashion to cling to what they have so crudely amputated, but . . . the Acropolis Museum has hit on the happy idea of exhibiting . . . its own original sculptures with the

London-held pieces represented by beautifully copied casts. This creates a natural thirst to see the actual re-assembly completed. So, <u>far from **emptying or weakening** a museum, this controversy has created another [museum], which is destined to be among Europe's **finest** galleries.</u> And one day, surely, there will be an agreement to do the right thing by the world's most "right" structure.

3. Similes / metaphors / allusions (implications) / synecdoche: 직유법, 비유 표현, 은유법 및 대유법을 사용하여 강조 효과를 내는 요소이다. 일반적 사람들이 잘 알고 있는 상징성 있는 개념을 활용하여 특정 사람이나 사물 또는 상황이 강하게 인식되도록 하는 방식이다.

> 예1: ('Apprenticeship' 지문의 경우는 이 스타일적 요소는 사용되지 않았다.)

> 예2: 'Parthenon' 지문에서는 'allusion'에 해당하는 요소가 밑줄 친 부분에 있다.

4.
. . . [T]here has been a bitter argument about the legitimacy of the British Museum's deal. I've written a whole book about this controversy and won't oppress you with all the details, but would just make this one point. <u>If the Mona Lisa had been sawed in two during the Napoleonic Wars and the separated halves had been acquired by different museums in, say, St. Petersburg and Lisbon, would there not be a general wish

to see what they might look like if re-united? If you think my analogy is overdrawn, consider this: the body of the goddess Iris is at present in London, while her head is in Athens. The front part of the torso of Poseidon is in London, and the rear part is in Athens. And so on. This is grotesque. . . .

7.

The British may continue in their constipated fashion to cling to what they have so crudely amputated, but . . . the Acropolis Museum has hit on the happy idea of exhibiting . . . its own original sculptures with the London-held pieces represented by beautifully copied casts. This creates a natural thirst to see the actual re-assembly completed. So, far from emptying or weakening a museum, this controversy has created another [museum], which is destined to be among Europe's finest galleries. And one day, surely, there will be an agreement to do the right thing by the world's most "right" structure.

4. Hyperbole / vivid language: 과장된 표현 또는 생생한 묘사적 표현을 사용하여 감성적 호소력을 높이는 요소로 쓰는 경우이다.

> 예1: ('Apprenticeship' 지문의 경우 이 요소라고 확정적으로 볼 수 있는 부분은 없다.)

> 예2: 'Parthenon' 지문에서는 이 요소가 상당히 많이 쓰였다고 할 수 있는데 다음의 밑줄 친 부분이다.

1.

The great classicist A. W. Lawrence . . . once remarked of the Parthenon that it is "the one building in the world which may be assessed as <u>absolutely right.</u>" . . .

2.

Not that the beauty and symmetry of the Parthenon have not been abused and <u>perverted and mutilated</u>. Five centuries after the birth of Christianity the Parthenon was closed and desolated. . . . Turkish forces also used it for centuries as a garrison and an arsenal, with the tragic result that in 1687 . . . a powder magazine was detonated and huge damage inflicted on the structure. <u>Most horrible of all</u>, perhaps, the Acropolis was made to fly a Nazi flag during the German occupation of Athens. . . .

3.

The damage done by the ages to the building, and by past empires and occupations, cannot all be put right. But there is one desecration and dilapidation that can at least be partially undone. Early in the 19th century, Britain's ambassador to the Ottoman Empire, Lord Elgin, sent a wrecking crew to the Turkish-occupied territory of Greece, where it sawed off approximately half of the adornment of the Parthenon and carried it away. As with all things Greek, there were three elements to this, the most lavish and beautiful sculptural treasury in human history. Under the direction of the artistic genius Phidias, the temple had two massive pediments decorated with the figures of Pallas Athena, Poseidon, and the gods of the sun and the moon. It then had a series of 92 high-relief panels, or metopes, depicting a succession of mythical and historical battles. The most intricate element was the frieze, carved in bas-relief, which showed the gods, humans, and animals that made up the annual Pan-Athens procession: there were 192 equestrian warriors and auxiliaries featured, which happens to be the exact number of the city's heroes who fell at the Battle of Marathon. Experts differ on precisely what story is being told here, but the frieze was quite clearly carved as a continuous narrative. Except that half the cast of the tale is still in Bloomsbury, in London, having been sold well below cost by Elgin to the British government in 1816 for $2.2 million in today's currency to pay off his many debts. . . .

4.

. . . [T]here has been a bitter argument about the legitimacy of the British Museum's deal. I've written a whole book about this controversy and won't oppress you with all the details, but would just make this one point. If the Mona Lisa had been sawed in two during the Napoleonic Wars and the separated halves had been acquired by different museums in, say, St. Petersburg and Lisbon, would there not be a general wish to see what they might look like if re-united? If you think my analogy is overdrawn, consider this: the body of the goddess Iris is at present in London, while her head is in Athens. The front part of the torso of Poseidon is in London, and the rear part is in Athens. And so on. <u>This is grotesque</u>. . . .

5.

It is unfortunately true that [Athens] allowed itself to become very dirty and polluted in the 20th century, and as a result the remaining sculptures and statues on the Parthenon were <u>nastily eroded</u> by "acid rain." . . . But gradually and now impressively, the Greeks have been living up to their responsibilities. Beginning in 1992, the endangered marbles were removed from the temple, given careful cleaning with ultraviolet and infrared lasers, and placed in a limate-controlled interior. . . .

7.

The British may continue in their constipated fashion to cling to what they have <u>so crudely amputated</u>, but . . . the Acropolis Museum has hit on the happy idea of exhibiting . . . its own original sculptures with the London-held pieces represented by beautifully copied casts. This creates a natural thirst to see the actual re-assembly completed. So, far from emptying or weakening a museum, this controversy has created another [museum], which is <u>destined to be among Europe's finest galleries</u>. And one day, surely, there will be an agreement to do the right thing by the world's most "right" structure.

5. Rhetorical questions: '수사적 의문' 또는 '반어적 의문'으로 형태만 question이고 사실상 statement인 경우를 쓰는 스타일이다. 답을 요구하는 질문이 아닌 '뻔한' 답이 나올 것을 예상한 상태로 질문을 던져 강조 효과를 내는 것이다.

> 예1: ('Apprenticeship' 지문의 경우 이 요소는 사용되지 않았다.)

> 예2: 'Parthenon' 지문에서는 한 부분에 이 요소가 쓰였는데 다음의 밑줄 친 부분이다.

4.

. . . [T]here has been a bitter argument about the legitimacy of the British Museum's deal. I've written a whole book about this controversy and won't oppress you with all the details, but would just make this one point. <u>If the Mona Lisa had been sawed in two during the Napoleonic Wars and the separated halves had been acquired by different museums in, say, St. Petersburg and Lisbon, would there not be a general wish to see what they might look like if re-united?</u> If you think my analogy is overdrawn, consider this: the body of the goddess Iris is at present in London, while her head is in Athens. The front part of the torso of Poseidon is in London, and the rear part is in Athens. And so on. This is grotesque. . . .

 **작성 트레이닝:**

이러한 분석을 기반으로 하여 답안의 본론 부분의 셋째 paragraph – styles 관련 단락을 작성해 보면 다음과 같다.

우선 'Apprenticeship'의 경우:

> *Finally, with respect to the stylistic elements used, contrast is the prominent feature that the author used.* Right from the beginning, he contrasts the practices of 'many business' in America which do not practice apprenticeships with those who "support apprenticeship programs." Then, he actually uses the word 'contrast' at the beginning of the 3rd paragraph as an indication that the U.S. falls far behind in the use of apprenticeships when compared with others. His expression in the 1st paragraph 'entirely overlooked' is juxtaposed with 'highly involved' in the 3rd paragraph; this is related to the contrasting situations between the U.S. and other European nations with respect to the unemployment rates. In paragraph 4, he also points out that "The U.S. is headed in the opposite direction. The number of apprenticeship programs has fallen", which is in contrast to what happened in Europe. These opposing lines of contents presented in his essay surely strengthen the emotional appeal in his message.

그리고 'Parthenon'의 경우 다음과 같이 작성해 볼 수 있다:

Lastly, when it comes to the stylistic elements, Hitchens turns to the use of allusion; he makes reference to 'Mona Lisa', which is readily recognized by people as a masterpiece preserved in one piece. In paragraph 4, he tosses a rhetorical question that, if 'Mona Lisa' had been sawed in two a long time ago and the separated halves had been in different museums … would there not be a general wish to see what they might look like if reunited?" He asks the readers and makes them stop to think, strengthening the appeal of his argument. To prove that his analogy is not outrageous, Hitchens describes how 'grotesque' the fact that the body of Iris and the front part of the torso of Poseidon are in London and Iris's head and the back portion of Poseidon's torso are in Athens is. *Furthermore, vivid language and contrasts are also adopted in the author's writing.* Throughout the article, the author chooses highly detailed and sometimes a bit exaggerated expressions, such as 'horrible, desecration, grotesque, crudely amputated, destined to be…', etc. Then, his quote from the classicist at the beginning that Parthenon is "absolutely right," is sharply contrasted it with the description in the following paragraph 2 that it is "Not [right] that the beauty and symmetry of the Parthenon have been abused…" This strong contrast with vivid expressions serves as a strong emotional plea for the readers. In paragraph 3, the author effectively contrasts what has been done in the past with those in more recent years; even though the damage the building has suffered from the ages, past empires and occupations "cannot all be put right", "one… can be partially undone". In the last paragraph 7, he pits the possibility of "emptying or weakening a museum" against "[creating] another [museum], which is destined to be among Europe's finest galleries," and concludes that this will eventually lead to "[doing] the right thing…" These stylistic components increase the level of emotional appeal of his message to the readers about returning the pieces to Greece.

트레이너 Tip:

- Evidences나 reasoning 부분과 중복되는 경우가 많으나 초점이 styles에 있으므로 전혀 문제되지 않으니 주저할 것 없이 전부 작성하면 된다.

- 미묘한 차이로 simile와 metaphor 등이 구분되므로 주의를 기울여 정확히 분석해야 이 부분에 대해 높은 점수를 받을 수 있다는 점을 기억할 것! (예: similar to, as, like 등의 표현이 있으면 simile, 없으면 metaphor가 되는 경우.) 이러한 경우들이 복합적으로 한 단락 안에서 쓰일 수도 있고, 또 allusion의 경우 metaphor와의 구분도 쉽지 않을 수 있는데, 사용되는 표현이 역사적, 학술적, 또는 사회적으로 유명한 case라서 굳이 관련 설명을 하지 않아도 자연스럽게 suggestive ideas가 전달된다면 allusion으로 생각하면 된다. (* 참고: 'simile' 발음 주의 – '시밀리'!)

- 'Synecdoche'(대유법)의 경우 '대표성이 있는 일부분에 비유하여 전체에서의 위치를 비유적으로 나타내는 경우인데,' 쓰이는 경우가 많지 않아도 마음속의 준비를 해둔다면 유용할 것이다. 예: "Marketing department is the bread and butter of this company."('bread and butter'가 차려진 식탁의 대표적 요소이므로 가장 중요한 기능을 이렇게 강조할 수 있음.) 에세이가 아닌 문학작품에 주로 쓰여 역시 빈도는 낮으나 allegory(우화, 풍자)도 있을 수 있으니 생각해 두면 좋겠다. (대표적 예는 George Orwell의 소설 'Animal Farm'에서 동물로 Russian society의 여러 단면을 풍자한 경우이다.)

- 두 가지 이상의 요소가 복합적으로 적용된 부분도 있을 수 있으므로 그 가능성을 염두에 두고 분석하면 더 효율적으로 완전한 답을 작성할 수 있음도 기억할 것!

Analysis 부분을 접근하는 방식에 대한 추가적 트레이너 Tip:

인터넷으로 검색을 하면 new SAT essay sample로 제시된 예들에서 흔히 볼 수 있는 format은 Aristotle의 'On Rhetoric'에 기초한 **'Logos, Pathos, Ethos'** 개념을 사용하여 분석과 작성의 체계로 삼는 것인데(이는 대략적으로 'logic, emotion, ethics'와 일치한다.), 그러나 필자의 입장에서 이는 권할 사항이 못 된다. 그 이유는 우선 그 시스템의 원래 목적이 문학작품을 이해하는 체계 – paradigm이기 때문에 사회적 현상 등에 대한 사실적 주장을 분석하는 데에 있어 목적과 부합하지 않는 면이 있고, 그보다 더 큰 이유는 너무 흔하게 쓰여서 자칫하면 외워서 쓴 것으로 채점자들에게 오해받을 수 있는데 그럴 경우 좋은 평가를 받을 수 없기 때문이다.

꼭 그 방식을 쓰고자 하는 특별한 이유가 있지 않는 한 조금 더 '자연스러운' 방식인 이 책에서 제시되는 format을 쓰기 바란다. 다음 Chapter에서 소개될 'templates'는 제시되는 몇 가지를 적절히 섞어서 준비하면 자신만의 독특한 form이 완성될 수 있는 것이다!

Chapter 04

텍플릿을 준비하라
- Have your 'template' ready!
+ How to make your 'own' template.

CHAPTER 04
SAT Essay - Template 활용법

여기서 잠깐!

이제까지 설명된 이해와 분석을 한 페이지로 정리하고 넘어가자 - 한눈에 보는 SAT-Essay 답안 구성은 다음과 같다.

Intro:

- Briefly summarize the author's argument + list the strategies, reasoning, and styles used.

Body:

A. Evidences - 전략적 요소:

- Use of statistics: 각종 통계적 사실을 인용하는 경우
- citing case studies: 잘 알려진 또는 학술적으로 연구된 사례를 인용하는 경우
- Reference to authorities: 권위가 있는 전문가나 지도자, 또는 기관의 의견이나 주장을 언급하는 경우

B. Reasoning aspects - 논리적 요소:

- Consequential / cause-effect reasoning: 원인-결과 등에 초점을 둔 논리적 기반
- Recognizing counter-arguments, but pointing out the logical flaws in them: 반대 의견의 논리적 문제점을 지적하는 논리적 접근
- Moral / ethical reasoning based on norms or basic principles of social systems 사회의 도덕적 또는 윤리적 가치관, 또는 민주주의, 자본주의의 원칙 등에 기초한 논리

C. Stylistic elements - 스타일적 요소:

- Personal anecdotes + first person language / perspectives: 개인적 일화 소개 및 1인칭 관점의 언어 사용
- Contrasts / parallelism / repetitions: 대조, 병치, 반복 등을 통하여 강조 효과를 내는 방법
- Similes / metaphors / allusions (implications) / synecdoche: 직유나 은유법을 통하여 효과적인 이미지나 감성을 전달하는 방법
- Hyperbole / vivid language: 과장법이나 생생한 표현으로 기술하는 부분
- Rhetorical questions: 수사적 질문으로 경각심을 일으키는 방법
- Recap. the author's argument + list the strategies, reasoning, and styles used one more time.

Conclusion:
- Recap. the author's argument + list the strategies, reasoning, and styles used one more time.

분석이 끝나고 Outline이 준비되면 이제 작성을 하여야 되는데, 이 과정은 지문 및 분석의 내용과 상관없이 미리 어느 정도 준비될 수 있는 부분이다. - 정해진 양식, 즉 'Template'을 준비해 놓고 그에 따라 작성하는 것이다.

본인만의 잘 준비된 Template을 활용한다면 Writing 점수에 도움이 되는 올바른 문법과 어법으로 작성하는 데 도움이 되며 또한 시간을 절약하는 효과적인 작성이 이루어질 수 있는 것이다.

* SAT - Essay Templates
(Try to build your own as you practice!)

Template 1:

> **Introduction**
> The article by (author) addresses the issue of (topic). In delivering his/her message to the readers / audience, the author chose to employ ------, ------, and ------- (specify the components of evidences, reasoning, and styles used), rendering his/her argument about (brief summary of the argument here) highly persuasive.

Body 1

Regarding the evidences, (the author)'s approach was the use of _____.

(+ Examples)

Then, (the author) also uses _____. (+ Examples)

+ These strategies render his/her argument logically very strong.

Body 2

Next, in terms of the reasoning involved, (the author) employs _____.

(+ Examples)

Moreover, he/she also chooses to _____. (+ Examples)

+ These reasoning aspects strengthens the convincingness of his/her argument.

Body 3

Finally, with respect to the stylistic elements, _____ is the prominent feature that the author used. (+ Examples)

Furthermore, _____ is also used. (+ Examples)

+ These stylistic elements boost the emotional appeal of his/her message to the readers / audience.

Conclusion

Hence, (the author)'s argument is carefully and eloquently constructed with ------, ------, and ------ (specify the components of evidences, reasoning, and styles used). Together, these elements effectively resulted in delivering a clear and persuasive argument to the readers / audience that (brief summary of the argument here).

Template 2:

Instruction

The topic of the article by (the author) is (topic) which is an important issue for our society. In presenting his/her argument to the readers / audience, the author relied on ------, ------, and ------- (specify the components of evidences, reasoning, and styles used), ensuring the persuasiveness in his/her argument that (brief summary of the argument here).

Body 1

When the evidences in the passage are examined, the author's strategy in presenting argument is the use of _____. (+ Examples)
Then, (the author) also utilizes _____. (+ Examples)

+ These strategies render his/her argument logically very strong.

Body 2

Then, when the reasoning aspect is scrutinized, (the author) relied on _____.
(+ Examples)
Moreover, he/she also chooses to _____. (+ Examples)

+ These reasoning aspects buttress the persuasiveness of his/her argument.

Body 3

Lastly, when it comes to the stylistic elements, (the author) uses _____.
(+ Examples)

Furthermore, _____ is also adopted in the author's writing.
(+ Examples)

+ These stylistic components increases the level of emotional appeal of his/her message to the readers / audience.

Conclusion

(the author)'s argument is elaborately and skillfully constructed with -------, -------, and ------- (specify the components of evidences, reasoning, and styles used). By utilizing these components in his/her argument, the author successfully delivered a clear and convincing message to the readers / audience that (brief summary of the argument here).

트레이너 Tip:

- 여기 제시된 두 templates를 적절히 혼합하여 '자신만의 format'을 준비하는 것이 더 좋다. 예를 들어 Template 1에서 intro와 conclusion 부분의 표현을 이용하고, 나머지 본문 부분은 Template 2에 있는 표현을 쓰는 식으로. 또한 표현의 일부를 대체하여 변화를 주어도 물론 괜찮을 것이다. (예를 들어 'scrutinized' → 'carefully analyzed', 'aspects' → 'facets', 'when it comes to' → 'concerning' 등으로.) 다만 바꾼 표현이 문법적으로, 의미적으로 적절한지 확인한 후 기억에 '정착'시키기 바란다.

- 이러한 준비된 pattern을 반복해서 쓰다 보면 자신도 모르게 이거 좀 바꿔야 되는 것이 아닌가라는 생각이 들 수 있지만, 논리적으로 생각하라. - 자신은 그 형식을 반복적으로 쓰고 있다는 걸 인식하지만 채점자는 그 사실을 알 수 없는 것이다. 따라서 그것은 옛말에 있는 "도둑이 제 발 저리다"라는 경우이니 여의치 말고 똑같은 표현을 써서 시간을 절약하고 실수를 줄이도록 하라!

 **작성 트레이닝:**

여기서 제시된 Template 1을 사용하여 'Apprenticeship' 지문에 대한 답을 작성한다면 다음과 같다:

> Peter Downs writes "Can't find Skilled Workers? Start an Apprentice Program" in an attempt to persuade the readers *that businesses in the U.S. should take advantage of apprenticeships in their employment practices.* Throughout the passage, Downs projects a strong message about implementing apprenticeships by using statistical data, concrete cases, cause-effect reasoning, and contrasts. These strategic, reasoning, and stylistic elements in his article buttress the persuasiveness of his argument to the readers about the merits of apprenticeship.

Regarding the strategies, Downs's first approach is the use of statistical data. He refers to numerous statistics throughout his essay regarding the benefits of apprenticeships for businesses. In paragraph 3, he points out that "In Switzerland, 70% of young people aged 15-19 apprentice in hundreds of occupations... In Germany, 65% of youth...; in Austria 55%. All three countries have youth unemployment rates less than half of America's 16%." Then, in the 4th paragraph, he presents the data about the differences between the U.S. and England by describing that "With only 330,578 registered apprentices..., the U.S. had less than 40% of the number in Britain..." Later in the essay, he presents the differences between the high-school students who go through apprenticeship and those who don't; "The mean grade point average for these students was 1.7 at the end of their sophomore year... By senior year, it was 3.13." Then, the author also cites actual cases to further strengthen the trustworthiness, and thus the logical quality of his argument. Downs introduces the case of an entrepreneur Jim McKelvey who successfully induced companies like 'Enterprise, Monsanto and Rawlings'... as a way to back up the benefits of apprenticeship. He elaborates on the program that these enterprises established, called 'LanuchCode,' which takes in people with just basic programming skills and trains them to be coders... Downs further cites the fact that "the U.S. Office for Apprenticeships has registered new apprenticeship programs in information technology, healthcare, [etc.]" Then, in paragraph 9, the positive impacts of apprenticeship programs on the academic performances of young students in the "Bayless School District in suburban St. Louis" were referred to as a specific case. *These statistical data and references to actual cases boost the credibility of the author's message*.

Next, in terms of the reasoning involved, the author basically offers the consequential reasoning regarding the benefits of apprenticeship programs, and how they can be the solution for some U.S. businesses that cannot find enough skilled workers. **In the 3rd paragraph, when he describes that differences between the U.S. and the European countries regarding the use of apprenticeships, the reasoning is that the U.S. businesses should also reap the benefits by following the Europeans. Also, in paragraph 4, when he cites the actual cases, his logic is essentially that those programs bring huge benefits for the companies that use apprenticeship programs. Then, Downs also turned to the cause-effect reasoning when he explained the effects of the program on the students who go through the apprenticeships; he offers elaborate explanations on how being in the program 'causes' the students to see the connection between what they learn and what they may be doing in their future jobs, resulting in the 'effects' of motivating them and boosting their attendance records and GPAs.** <u>Together, these reasoning elements buttress the logical appeal of his message.</u>

Lastly, with respect to the stylistic elements used, contrast is the prominent feature that the author used. Right from the beginning, he contrasts the practices of 'many businesses' in America which do not practice apprenticeships with those who "support apprenticeship programs." Then, he actually uses the word 'contrast' at the beginning of the 3rd paragraph as an indication that the U.S. falls far behind in the use of apprenticeships when compared with others. His expression in the 1st paragraph 'entirely overlooked' is juxtaposed with 'highly involved' in the 3rd paragraph; this is related to the contrasting situations between the U.S. and other European nations with respect to the unemployment rates. In paragraph 4, he also points out that "The U.S. is headed in the opposite direction. The number of apprenticeship programs has fallen", which is in contrast to what happened in Europe. <u>These opposing lines of contents presented in his essay surely strengthen the emotional appeal in his message.</u>

The author effectively used exact data, concrete cases, consequential and cause-effect reasoning, and contrasts in his essay. Together, these strategies resulted in successfully persuading the readers that *the practice of apprenticeship should be much more frequently and eagerly implemented by businesses in the U.S.*

(Word count: 764)

이번에는 Template 2를 사용하여 'Parthenon' 지문에 대한 답을 작성해 보면 다음과 같다:

Christopher Hitchens writes "The Lovely Stones" in an attempt to persuade the audience that the original sculptures from the Parthenon must be returned to Greece. Throughout the passage, Hitchens projects a strong message about the sculptures' relocation through, historical and statistical data, moral reasoning, allusion, vivid language, and contrast. These elements and strategies certainly buttress the persuasiveness of his argument to the readers.

When the evidences in the article are examined, the author's strategy in presenting argument is making references to exact historical and current data to beef up the logical quality of his argument. He first describes Parthenon with highly detailed references to its features like, "92 high-relief panels," "192 equestrian warriors and auxiliaries," etc. Then he points to the injustice by describing the fact that the precious pieces of the structure were "sold well below cost by Elgin to the British government in 1816 for $2.2 million in today's currency" which is a small amount for a great historical treasure. He also mentions how the Greeks saved the remaining sculptures and statues and are preserving their beauty in a museum away from the dangerous effects of the elements, "[w]ith 10 times the space of the old repository, it display[s] all the marvels that go with the temples on top of the hill..." His descriptions of how Greeks are treating the sculptures right "with ultraviolet and infra-red lasers..." offer realistic pictures about what should be done. Together, these detailed and factual references strengthen the logical appeal of his message.

Then, when the reasoning aspect is scrutinized, the author relied mostly on the moral reasoning. Hitchens used the word 'right' several times throughout his essay, which is the indication that he is mostly relying on reminding people of what is the morally the desirable action to be taken regarding the issue. Right from the beginning in paragraph 1, he quotes the great classicist A. W. Lawrence's statement "the one building in the world which may be assessed as absolutely right.". In the last paragraph, the author describes the consensus among nations involved regarding the return of the sculptures to Greece as "agreement to do the right thing by the world's most "right" structure." Then, he describes what have been "done by past empires and occupations…" as "desecration and dilapidation", indicating that they were wrong and thus must be "undone" by returning the pieces to Greece. <u>These reasoning aspects also buttress the persuasiveness of his argument</u>.

Lastly, when it comes to the stylistic elements, Hitchens turns to the use of allusion; he makes reference to 'Mona Lisa', which is readily recognized by people as a masterpiece preserved in one piece. In paragraph 4, he tosses a rhetorical question that, if 'Mona Lisa' had been sawed in two a long time ago and the separated halves had been in different museums ... would there not be a general wish to see what they might look like if reunited?" He asks the readers and makes them stop to think, strengthening the appeal of his argument. To prove that his analogy is not outrageous, Hitchens describes how 'grotesque' the fact that the body of Iris and the front part of the torso of Poseidon are in London and Iris's head and the back portion of Poseidon's torso are in Athens is. Furthermore, vivid language and contrasts are also adopted in the author's writing. Throughout the article, the author chooses highly detailed and somewhat exaggerated expressions, such as 'horrible, desecration, grotesque, crudely amputated, destined to be...', etc. Then, his quote from the classicist at the beginning that Parthenon is "absolutely right," is sharply contrasted it with the description in the following paragraph 2 that it is "Not [right] that the beauty and symmetry of the Parthenon have been abused..." This strong contrast with vivid expressions serves as a strong emotional plea for the readers. In paragraphs 3, the author effectively contrasts what has been done in the past with those in more recent years; even though the damage the building has suffered from the ages, past empires and occupations "cannot all be put right", "one... can be partially undone". In the last paragraph 7, he pits the possibility of "emptying or weakening a museum" against "[creating] another [museum], which is destined to be among Europe's finest galleries," and concludes that this will eventually lead to "[doing] the right thing..." *These stylistic components increase the level of emotional appeal of his message to the readers about returning the pieces to Greece.*

Hitchens's argument is elaborately and skillfully constructed with exact data, moral reasoning, allusion, vivid language, and contrast. *By utilizing these components in his argument, the author successfully delivered a clear and convincing message to the readers regarding the righteousness of returning the original stones of Parthenon to Greece.*

(Word count: 788)

Chapter 05

하지 말아야 할 것들
vs. 해야 할 것들
- What NOT to do vs. what to do!
Learning through the
comparisons between some
'bad' essays and 'good' ones!

CHAPTER 05
하지 말아야 할 것들 vs. 해야 할 것들
– What NOT to do vs. what to do!

이 장에서는 SAT-Essay 작성에 있어 '하지 말아야 할 것'에 대하여 설명해 보도록 하겠다. Bad sample을 분석해 보며 왜 그것이 적절한 답이 아닌지 생각해 보고, 이어서 그에 상응하는 Good sample들을 보면 여러분들이 적절한 답을 작성하는 데 있어 무엇을 해야 하는지가 더욱 더 확실히 보일 것이다.

여기서 잠깐!

일단 각 Bad vs. Good samples를 보기 전 해당 지문에 대하여 50분간 여러분 스스로 에세이 답안을 작성한 후 설명을 읽기 바란다. (실전 시험이라 생각하고 긴장감 있게 시도해야 이해가 잘될 것이다!) 훨씬 더 효과적인 '깨달음'이 있을 것이다 – 시험에서 한 번 틀린 문제를 나중에 또 틀리는 일은 거의 없다는 것을 기억하라!

Practice for Bad vs. Good essays #1:

* Source: John F. Kennedy's speech, September 12, 1962. Rice Stadium, Houston, TX

(Retrieved online through: https://www.jfklibrary.org/asset-viewer/archives/JFKPOF/040/JFKPOF-040-001)

As you read the passage below, consider how President John F. Kennedy uses

- evidence, such as facts or examples, to support claims.
- reasoning to develop ideas and to connect claims and evidence.
- stylistic or persuasive elements, such as word choice or appeals to emotion, to add power to the ideas expressed.

1.

We set sail on this new sea because there is new knowledge to be gained, and new rights to be won, and they must be won and used for the progress of all people. For space science, like nuclear science and all technology, has no conscience of its own. Whether it will become a force for good or ill depends on man, and only if the United States occupies a position of pre-eminence can we help decide whether this new ocean will be a sea of peace or a new terrifying theater of war. I do not say that we should or will go unprotected against the hostile misuse of space any more than we go unprotected against the hostile use of land or sea, but I do say that space can be explored and mastered without feeding the fires of war, without repeating the mistakes that man has made in extending his writ around this globe of ours.

2.

There is no strife, no prejudice, no national conflict in outer space as yet. Its hazards are hostile to us all. Its conquest deserves the best of all mankind, and its opportunity for peaceful cooperation may never come again. But why, some say, the moon? Why choose this as our goal? And they may well ask why climb the highest mountain? Why, 35 years ago, fly the Atlantic? Why does Rice play Texas?

3.

We choose to go to the moon. We choose to go to the moon in this decade and do the other things, not because they are easy, but because they are hard, because that goal will serve to organize and measure the best of our energies and skills, because that challenge is one that we are willing to accept, one we are unwilling to postpone, and one which we intend to win, and the others, too.

4.

It is for these reasons that I regard the decision last year to shift our efforts in space from low to high gear as among the most important decisions that will be made during my incumbency in the office of the Presidency…

5.

To be sure, we are behind, and will be behind for some time in manned flight. But we do not intend to stay behind, and in this decade, we shall make up and move ahead.

6.

The growth of our science and education will be enriched by new knowledge of our universe and environment, by new techniques of learning and mapping and observation, by new tools and computers for industry, medicine, the home as well as the school. Technical institutions, such as Rice, will reap the harvest of these gains.

7.

And finally, the space effort itself, while still in its infancy, has already created a great number of new companies, and tens of thousands of new jobs. Space and related industries are generating new demands in investment and skilled personnel, and this city and this State, and this region, will share greatly in this growth. What was once the furthest outpost on the old frontier of the West will be the furthest outpost on the new frontier of science and space. Houston, your City of Houston, with its Manned Spacecraft Center, will become the heart of a large scientific and engineering community. During the next 5 years the National Aeronautics and Space Administration expects to double the number of scientists and engineers in this area, to increase its outlays for salaries and expenses to $60 million a year; to invest some $200 million in plant and laboratory facilities; and to direct or contract for new space efforts over $1 billion from this Center in this City…

8.

Many years ago the great British explorer George Mallory, who was to die on Mount Everest, was asked why did he want to climb it. He said, "Because it is there."

9.

Well, space is there, and we're going to climb it, and the moon and the planets are there, and new hopes for knowledge and peace are there. And, therefore, as we set sail we ask God's blessing on the most hazardous and dangerous and greatest adventure on which man has ever embarked.

Write an essay in which you explain how President Kennedy builds an argument to expand and move forward with the United States' space program. In your essay, analyze how Kennedy uses one or more of the features listed above (or features of your own choice) to strengthen the logic and persuasiveness of his argument. Be sure that your analysis focuses on the most relevant aspects of the passage.

Your essay should not explain whether you agree with Kennedy's claims, but rather explain how the author builds an argument to persuade his audience.

A.

The 'bad' sample first!

다음의 Bad sample essay는 크게 두 가지 측면에서 bad essay라고 할 수 있다.

1. 역시 작성자 본인의 의견이 첫 body paragraph의 주 내용이다. 그 대신 speech의 주제를 잘 정리하고 JFK가 어떤 논리로 메시지를 전하고 있는지를 설명했어야 한다. (이 내용 대신 space exploration에 대한 연구를 지원할 경우 그 결과로 얻을 수 있는 기술 발전 및 경제적 파급효과, 그리고 반대 의견을 인정하고 그에 대한 체계적 반박을 제공하는 식으로 자신의 주장의 설득력을 높인점이 설명됐어야 한다.)

2. 두 번째 body paragraph에서 statistics 관련하여 본문에서 해당되는 예를 충분히 들지 않아서 analysis 점수를 충분히 받지 못하는 essay가 되었다. Economic benefits에 대하여 JFK가 언급한 내용을 quote하면서 자세히 설명했어야 한다.

다만 이 경우 Writing 부분 점수는 7점 정도로 잘 나올 수 있는, 문법이나 표현상의 실수는 거의 없는 essay이다.

A bad sample on:

"Speech at Rice Stadium" by John F. Kennedy

The former President Kennedy was not only one of the most popular presidents of the U.S., but also one of the best speech makers. His eloquent speech at Rice Stadium on the then controversial decision to allocate tax revenues for building a preeminent space program was one of the proofs. I wholeheartedly agree with this view that was presented with supporting evidences and using powerful metaphors; his view was indeed eloquently presented.

Former president J. F. Kennedy's argument that the U.S. government should *continue the support for the space exploration program was surely a praiseworthy message. I always felt that space exploration is critical in ensuring the scientific and technological power of a nation, and thus I have to say that he was really wise in persuading the American public at the time regarding the need to support the activities and investments therein. I was also impressed by his insight that expanding space programs will also bring numerous economic and social benefits; indeed, I believe that the economy of the Texas area improved back then, and the solidarity of the people in the Houston area grew after the implementation of the programs.*

JFK's main approach in presenting his points persuasively is the use of supporting evidences. The first example of supporting evidence he utilizes is his reference to the statistics of the U.S. government; part of the argument for that investment had been that nuclear technology could be used by the United States for its own benefit and protection, or against the United States by foreign nations who may intend harm. In doing this, JFK draws a parallel between nuclear weapons and space exploration; "Whether [space exploration becomes] a force for good or ill depends on man, and only if the United States occupies a position of pre-eminence can we help decide [the future of space]." Kennedy also cites economic data to further support argument. These render his speech worthwhile to listen to.

Next, JFK turns to the use of various metaphors to strengthen his argument. His metaphors are woven throughout his address. Kennedy states that "We set sail on this new sea." This metaphor has the effect of emphasizing the fact that space exploration will expand the breadth of current science and *technology. Kennedy continues the sea metaphor by saying that space may become "a sea of peace or a new terrifying theater of war," as he suggests that the position of the United States in space exploration may decide the nature of this new frontier. Kennedy also analogously describes Houston as "once the furthest outpost on the old frontier of the West" in order to call the listener's mind to the nature of change over time. Houston looked essentially nothing like the Houston of the old West, and this metaphor provokes the listener's rich imagination. These metaphors effectively serve to evoke strong emotional responses with emphatic effects.*

Overall, JFK's argument was very convincing; I totally agree with his view that space exploration should be fully supported for the sake of the nation and possibly for the world. By using various techniques, I believe he really succeeded delivering a 'historic' speech.

(Word count: 525)

B.

Now the 'good' one!

앞서 Bad essay로 제시된 것을 고쳐서 이상적으로 쓴다면 있어서는 안 될 요소들을 빼고 대신 더 정확한(subjective하지 않고 objective한), 그리고 완전한 분석 요소들을 넣어 다음과 같이 작성하면 좋은 Essay가 되는 것이다!

A good sample on:

"Speech at Rice Stadium" by John F. Kennedy

Rarely anyone would deny the fact that the former President Kennedy was a master speech maker. His eloquent speech at Rice Stadium on the then controversial decision to allocate tax revenues for building a preeminent space program was one of the proofs. **By providing** supporting evidences, acknowledging and addressing the concerns of those dubious about the idea of space exploration, and using powerful metaphors, Kennedy **crafted a powerful and memorable speech.**

Regarding the evidences, former president J. F. Kennedy's **approach in presenting his points persuasively is** the use of supporting evidences. The first example of supporting evidence he utilizes is his reference to the fact that the United States had invested significantly in the development of nuclear technology; part of the argument for that investment had been that nuclear technology could be used by the United States for its own benefit and protection, or against the United States by foreign nations who may intend harm. In doing this, JFK draws a parallel between nuclear weapons and space exploration; "Whether [space exploration becomes] a force for good or ill depends on man, and only if the United States occupies a position of pre-eminence can we help decide [the future of space]." A further piece of evidence Kennedy uses is the example of flight across the Atlantic; he reminds his audience of this event in order to reference a previous accomplishment that had also once been seen as prohibitively difficult, but proven to be useful later in many ways. Kennedy also cites economic data, filling the last part of his speech with specific economic benefits for the Houston area, including the doubling of the number of scientists and engineers hired and the public spending of $60 million per year. **These points together render his speech worthwhile to listen to and credible.**

With respect to the reasoning elements involved, John E. Kennedy **used** the approach of acknowledging counter-arguments to fortify the persuasiveness of his argument. By asking "But why, some say, the moon?" Rather than dismissing this point as irrelevant, Kennedy seeks to disarm it by embracing the potential skeptics' view and pointing to some great historical achievements which invited similar doubts. By citing questions, "[why] climb the highest mountain" and [why] "fly the Atlantic," JFK tries to establish the value of the trip to the moon which will become obvious later. **He continues to acknowledge** this potential objection by saying that the goal has been chosen "because [it is] hard," and therefore will "serve to organize and measure the best of our energies and skills." Another counterargument Kennedy addresses is that "we are behind…in manned flight." Again, Kennedy chose to affirm the objection by stating "we…will be behind for some time". **These acknowledgements give the sense of objectivity and balance in his speech, making it more appealing to the audience.**

Finally, in terms of the stylistic elements, JFK **relied on the use of** various metaphors **to strengthen his argument**. His metaphors are woven throughout his address. Kennedy states that "We set sail on this new sea." This metaphor serves to recall the listener's mind to a frontier that was once seen as unfathomably expansive and beyond human mastery. Kennedy continues the sea metaphor by saying that space may become "a sea of peace or a new terrifying theater of war," as he suggests that the position of the United States in space exploration may decide the nature of this new frontier. Kennedy also analogously describes Houston as "once the furthest outpost on the old frontier of the West" in order to call the listener's mind to the nature of change over time. Houston looked essentially nothing like the Houston of the old West, and this metaphor provokes the listener's imagination to project the possibilities for a new Houston, built on a strong space program. A third metaphor is used in a rhetorical question form and with repetitions; in paragraph 2, Kennedy asks "Why, 35 years ago, fly the Atlantic?" followed immediately by another question, "Why does Rice play Texas?" **Thus, these metaphors and repetitive rhetorical questions effectively evoke strong emotional responses.**

Overall, JFK's argument is carefully and eloquently constructed with strong supporting evidences, acknowledgement of counter-arguments, and the use of metaphors. **Together, I he succeeded in delivering a very persuasive and indeed a 'historic' speech to the audience.**

(Word count: 716)

다시 여기서 잠깐!

다음의 Bad vs. Good samples set를 보기 전 해당 지문에 대하여 실전 시험이라 생각하고 50분간 여러분 스스로 에세이 답안을 작성한 후 설명을 보기 바란다. – 이해가 훨씬 더 효과적일 것이다!

Practice for Bad vs. Good essays #2:

* Excerpt adapted from former U.S. President Jimmy Carter's foreword to Arctic National Wildlife Refuge: Seasons of Life and Land, a Photographic Journey, by Subhankar Banerjee, © 2003.

(Retrieved online through: https://mrbrownswhs.files.wordpress.com/2016/03/jimmy-carter-anwr.docx)

As you read the passage below, consider how the former President Jimmy Carter uses:

– evidence, such as facts or examples, to support claims.
– reasoning to develop ideas and to connect claims and evidence.
– stylistic or persuasive elements, such as word choice or appeals to emotion, to add power to the ideas expressed.

1.
The Arctic National Wildlife Refuge stands alone as America's last truly great wilderness. This magnificent area is as vast as it is wild, from the windswept coastal plain where polar bears and caribou give birth, to the towering Brooks Range where Dall sheep cling to cliffs and wolves howl in the midnight sun.

2.
More than a decade ago, [my wife] Rosalynn and I had the fortunate opportunity to camp and hike in these regions of the Arctic Refuge. During bright July days, we walked along ancient caribou trails and studied the brilliant mosaic of wildflowers, mosses, and lichens that hugged the tundra. There was a timeless quality about this great land. As the never-setting sun circled above the horizon, we watched muskox, those shaggy survivors of the Ice Age, lumber along braided rivers that meander toward the Beaufort Sea.

3.
One of the most unforgettable and humbling experiences of our lives occurred on the coastal plain. We had hoped to see caribou during our trip, but to our amazement, we witnessed the migration of tens of thousands of caribou with their newborn calves. In a matter of a few minutes, the sweep of tundra before us became flooded with life, with the sounds of grunting animals and clicking hooves filling the air. The dramatic procession of the Porcupine caribou herd was a once-in-a-lifetime wildlife spectacle. We understand firsthand why some have described this special birthplace as

"America's Serengeti."

4.

Standing on the coastal plain, I was saddened to think of the tragedy that might occur if this great wilderness was consumed by a web of roads and pipelines, drilling rigs and industrial facilities. Such proposed developments would forever destroy the wilderness character of America's only Arctic Refuge and disturb countless numbers of animals that depend on this northernmost terrestrial ecosystem.

5.

The extraordinary wilderness and wildlife values of the Arctic Refuge have long been recognized by both Republican and Democratic presidents. In 1960, President Dwight D. Eisenhower established the original 8.9 million-acre Arctic National Wildlife Range to preserve its unique wildlife, wilderness, and recreational values. Twenty years later, I signed the Alaska National Interest Lands Conservation Act, monumental legislation that safeguarded more than 100 million acres of national parks, refuges, and forests in Alaska. This law specifically created the Arctic National Wildlife Refuge, doubled the size of the former range, and restricted development in areas that are clearly incompatible with oil exploration.

6.

Since I left office, there have been repeated proposals to open the Arctic Refuge coastal plain to oil drilling. Those attempts have failed because of tremendous opposition by the American people, including the Gwich'in Athabascan Indians of Alaska and Canada, indigenous people whose culture has depended on the Porcupine caribou herd for thousands of years. Having visited many aboriginal peoples around the world, I can empathize with the Gwich'ins' struggle to safeguard one of their precious human rights.

7.
We must look beyond the alleged benefits of a short-term economic gain and focus on what is really at stake. At best, the Arctic Refuge might provide 1 to 2 percent of the oil our country consumes each day. We can easily conserve more than that amount by driving more fuel-efficient vehicles. Instead of tearing open the heart of our greatest refuge, we should use our resources more wisely.

8.
There are few places on earth as wild and free as the Arctic Refuge. It is a symbol of our national heritage, a remnant of frontier America that our first settlers once called wilderness. Little of that precious wilderness remains.

9.
It will be a grand triumph for America if we can preserve the Arctic Refuge in its pure, untrammeled state. To leave this extraordinary land alone would be the greatest gift we could pass on to future generations.

Write an essay in which you explain how Jimmy Carter builds an argument to persuade his audience that the Arctic National Wildlife Refuge should not be developed for industry. In your essay, analyze how Carter uses one or more of the features listed in the box above (or features of your own choice) to strengthen the logic and persuasiveness of his argument. Be sure that your analysis focuses on the most relevant features of the passage. Your essay should not explain whether you agree with Carter's claims, but rather explain how Carter builds an argument to persuade his audience.

A.
The 'bad' sample first!

이어서 다음의 Sample essay는 세 가지 측면에서 앞선 첫 경우보다도 더 bad essay라고 할 수 있다.

1. 작성자 본인의 의견이 '마구' 들어가 있다. - 마치 instruction이 'evaluate the argument of the author'인 것처럼... 마지막까지 자신이 설득을 받은 점을 main point of the answer로, 그것도 반복적으로 쓰고 있다.

2. 지문에서 쓰여진 main technique에 대한 언급이 빠져 있다. - analysis 측면에서 정확하고 충분하지 못한 essay인 것이다. 또한 일부 인용은 했지만 그것이 'vivid language'의 사용이라든가 'metaphor'였다는 등의 정확한 indentification이 없었다.

3. Writing 면에서도 좋은 평가를 받을 수 없다. - misspelling에서부터 usage에 맞지 않는 표현까지 작지만 채점자 입장에서 지나칠 수 없는 실수들이 너무 많다!

A bad sample on:

"Foreword to Arctic National Wildlife Refuge: Seasons of Life and Land, A Photographic Journey" by Jimmy Carter

We often see these messages from wildlife organizations. But this message was different. I was in total agreement with Jimmy Carter's opinion on preserving the Arctic National Wildlife Refuge". The former U.S. President's essay touched my heart; he provided some impressive evidences, personal stories in presenting his argument effectively.

I thought the way he presented the evidences were really professional. He noted that vast lands have been a designated: "8.9 million-acre" haven for wildlife since President Eisenhower established it in 1960. He added that he "signed the Alaska National Interest Lands Conservation Act". By mentioning these legislations that were important in the history of the U.S. and maybe the world, Carter convinced me that the effort to preserve wildlife is certainly the most righteous and important step that must be taken by our society and the international organizations. These evidences were quite enough to convince me and others in beleiving in him.

Moreover, I thought his **styles of writing was equally impresed. He provided some fun and colorful personal stories.** He describes what he saw as "One of the most unforgettable and humbling experiences of our lives." The fact that he was right there made me think that he truly felt the needs to protect the wildlife, instead of having political or any other motives. He states that "to our amazement, we witnessed the migration of tens of thousands of caribou with their newborn calves. He describes these so realistically that I felt like I was actually there, witnessing the scenes myself. That surely made me think about the value of reserving the 'pure' environment that we have in those refuge locations. Also when he describes all the details about the animals and nature that is so precious, and used the names like "America's Serengeti" which makes me think about the really beautiful scenery in Africa, I could not help but put myself in the position of preservationist and feel enthusiastic about participating in any future movements for wildlife and refuge preservations. His expressions were surely the best part of his article; they left a resting impression in my mineset.

Thus, Carter made me a believer in him. After reading his article, I felt that I should do my best to support the wildlife refuge preservation efforts as much as I could. I am sure that millions more are also persuaded to his message, and they will likely take some action to protect the wildlife.

(Word count: 408)

B. Now the 'good' one!

역시 이 경우에도 먼저 Bad essay로 제시된 것을 고쳐서 이상적으로 쓴다면 있어서는 안 될 요소들을 빼고 대신 더 완전한 분석 요소들을 포함시켜 다음과 같이 '더 길고 정확하게' 작성하면 되는 것이다!

A good sample on:

"Foreword to Arctic National Wildlife Refuge: Seasons of Life and Land, A Photographic Journey" by Jimmy Carter

Jimmy Carter's essay "Arctic National Wildlife Refuge" demands that each of America's citizens consider the environment as an integral part of their lives. The former U.S. President's essay skills help him make his points ring clear. He uses supporting evidences, consequential reasoning, personal eyewitness testimonies, and vivid and figurative languages to highlight the point that the Arctic National Wildlife Refuge "should not be developed for industry."

In terms of the evidences, the author provided supporting evidences, including some statistical data. He underscores his primary concerns for this Refuge by citing pertinent pieces of evidence which appeal to the readers. First, Carter notes that this land has been a designated "8.9 million-acre" haven for wildlife since President Eisenhower established it in 1960. He expounds upon this by adding that he "signed the Alaska National Interest Lands Conservation Act". By referencing to both of these legislations, Carter establishes a timeline for conservation which shows there is precedence for preserving the area in question. Carter goes on to explain that what the oil industries would gain from the region would not be enough of an amount to justify its destruction. He states that "we must look beyond the alleged benefits of a short-term economic gain" and points out that "at best, the Arctic Refuge might provide 1 to 2 percent of the oil our country consumes each day". Why would anyone pillage this environmental asset for such a small amount of oil? **These evidences collectively bolster the logical quality and persuasiveness of his argument.**

Regarding the reasoning aspect, Carter's approach in presenting his argument persuasively is through the consequential reasoning. In Paragraph 4, he points to the negative consequences by stating that "Such proposed developments would forever destroy the wilderness character of America's only Arctic Refuge and disturb countless numbers of animals that depend on this northernmost terrestrial ecosystem". **Then, he explained the relatively small economic benefits in order to persuade the readers that there is much more to lose when development is chosen over preservation.** In Paragraph 7, he points out that "At best, the Arctic Refuge might provide 1 to 2 percent of the oil our country consumes each day. He quickly followed it up with ideas for alternative efforts: "We can easily conserve more than that amount by driving more fuel-efficient vehicles." These reasoning aspects buttressed the logical appeal of his essay.

Finally, with respect to his styles, he turned to the use of personal anecdotes and vivid language. He describes what he saw as "One of the most unforgettable and humbling experiences of our lives." He continues by stating "to our amazement, we witnessed the migration of tens of thousands of caribou with their newborn calves. In a matter of a few minutes, the sweep of tundra before us became flooded with life, with the sounds of grunting animals and clicking hooves filling the air," while also adding to his descriptions with what he recalls as 'dramatic spectacles'. Essentially, he makes sure that the readers understand the beauty of the refuge by indicating that he and his wife could 'understand' why some call the area "America's Serengeti." **The emotional appeal of his message is boosted by these accounts. Also, Carter adopts intensely vivid and figurative language to strengthen the plea in his essay.** Carter first establishes beautiful imagery to map this arctic refuge in the reader's mind. From "the never-setting sun circled above the horizon" to "the sounds of grunting animals and clicking hooves filling the air," Carter vividly recreates the experience of being on this land to make readers feel connected to it, essentially underscoring its value in their minds. Then he uses expressions like "brilliant mosaic of wildflowers" and "muskox, those shaggy survivors of the Ice Age" to convey the gripping nature of the scenes the people can behold there. When Carter begins to conclude his essay in paragraph 7, he compares developing this region to "tearing open the heart." This metaphor which personifies the land with a painful, bloody and gut-wrenching act drives his message home. At the end of his essay, Carter metaphorically equates successful preservation with 'triumphs' and 'gift', too. **Together, these expressions powerfully increase the emotional appeal of his argument.**

Thus, Carter used evidences, consequential reasoning, persnal anecdotes, and 'photographic' and metaphorical expressions to present a powerful and effective message to the readers. **Together, these elements in his essay were highly effective in delivering a clear and persuasive argument to the readers** regarding the need to preserve the wildlife refuge.

(Word count: 750)

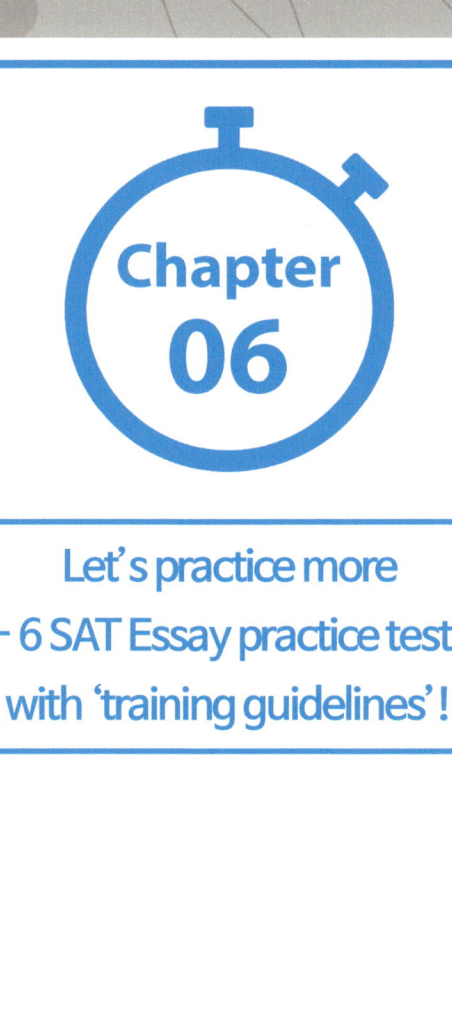

Chapter 06

Let's practice more
− 6 SAT Essay practice tests
with 'training guidelines'!

CHAPTER 06

Let's practice more
– 6 SAT Essay practice tests with 'training guidelines'!

지금까지 충실히 이 책의 '트레이닝'을 따라왔다면 이제 기본 실력이 어느 정도 갖추어졌을 것이다. 이 장에서는 마무리 트레이닝으로 **연습 문제 6회분**을 가지고 실전 준비를 해 보도록 하자.

일단 각 문제를 공부하기 전 실전이라는 마음가짐으로 50분간 최대한 노력하여 답안을 작성하여야 한다. 그리고 나서 문제에 따라 나오는 '트레이닝 Guideline'을 보면서 자신이 분석하고 작성한 에세이에 Guideline에 명시된 요소들이 다 포함되어 있는지 확인을 해 보면서 잘하고 잘 못한 부분에 대하여 '깨달음의 과정'을 거치면 된다. (고심하고 난 후 깨닫는 일종의 '소크라테스식 교육'이라고 생각하라!) 그리고 최종적으로 다시 한번 Guideline을 반영하면서 작성하여 봄으로 하여 확실한 실력 향상이 있도록 연습한다!

SAT-Essay-Practice Test #1:

Analyze and write about the following passage, following the instructions given at the end (50 minutes):

The reading passage is taken from Barbara Ehrenreich, "The Selfish Side of Gratitude" ©2015 by The New York Times Company. Originally published December 31, 2015.

* Retrieved online through:
  https://www.nytimes.com/2016/01/03/opinion/sunday/the-selfish-side-of-gratitude.html

1.
This holiday season, there was something in the air that was even more inescapable than the scent of pumpkin spice: gratitude.

2.
In November, NPR issued a number of brief exhortations to cultivate gratitude, culminating in an hourlong special on the "science of gratitude," narrated by Susan Sarandon. Writers in Time magazine, The New York Times, and Scientific American recommended it as a surefire ticket to happiness and even better health. Robert Emmons, a psychology professor at the University of California, Davis, who studies the "science of gratitude," argues that it leads to a stronger immune system and lower blood pressure, as well as "more joy and pleasure."

3.

It's good to express our thanks, of course, to those who deserve recognition. But this holiday gratitude is all about you, and how you can feel better.

Gratitude is hardly a fresh face on the self-improvement scene. By the turn of the century, Oprah Winfrey and other motivational figures were promoting an "attitude of gratitude." Martin Seligman, the father of "positive psychology," which is often enlisted to provide some sort of scientific basis for "positive thinking," has been offering instruction in gratitude for more than a decade…

4.

But positive thinking was in part undone by its own silliness, glaringly displayed in the 2006 bestseller "The Secret," which announced that you could have anything, like the expensive necklace you'd been coveting, simply by "visualizing" it in your possession.

The financial crash of 2008 further dimmed the luster of positive thinking, which had done so much to lure would-be homeowners and predatory mortgage lenders into a speculative frenzy. This left the self-improvement field open to more cautious stances, like mindfulness and resilience and — for those who could still muster it — gratitude.

…Perhaps it's no surprise that gratitude's rise to self-help celebrity status owes a lot to the…John Templeton Foundation. At the start of this decade, the foundation…gave $5.6 million to Dr. Emmons, the gratitude researcher. It also funded a $3 million initiative called Expanding the Science and Practice of Gratitude through the Greater Good Science Center at the University of California, Berkeley, which co-produced the special that aired on NPR. The foundation does not fund projects to directly improve the lives of poor individuals, but it has spent a great deal, through efforts like these, to improve their attitudes.

5.

Furthermore, it appears that much of the gratitude advice involves no communication or interaction of any kind. Consider this, from a yoga instructor on CNN.com: "Cultivate your sense of gratitude by incorporating giving thanks into a personal morning ritual such as writing in a gratitude journal, repeating an affirmation or practicing a meditation. It could even be as simple as writing what you give thanks for on a sticky note and posting it on your mirror or computer. To help you establish a daily routine, create a 'thankfulness' reminder on your phone or computer to pop up every morning and prompt you." Who is interacting here? "You" and "you."

6.

Yet there is a need for more gratitude, especially from those who have a roof over their heads and food on their table. Only it should be a more vigorous and inclusive sort of gratitude than what is being urged on us now. Who picked the lettuce in the fields, processed the standing rib roast, drove these products to the stores, stacked them on the supermarket shelves and, of course, prepared them and brought them to the table? ··· There are crowds, whole communities of actual people, many of them with aching backs and tenuous finances, who made the meal possible.

7.

The real challenge of gratitude lies in figuring out how to express our debt to them, whether through generous tips or, say, by supporting their demands for decent pay and better working conditions. But now we're not talking about gratitude, we're talking about a far more muscular impulse — and this is, to use the old-fashioned term, "solidarity" — which may involve getting up off the yoga mat.

Instruction

Write an essay in which you explain how Richard Schiffman *builds the argument. In your essay, analyze how the author uses one or more of the features of evidences, reasoning, and styles (or features of your own choice) to strengthen the logic and persuasiveness of his argument. Be sure that your analysis focuses on the most relevant aspects of the passage.*

Your essay should not explain whether you agree with the author's claims, but rather explain how the author builds an argument to persuade his audience.

∗ 트레이닝 Guidelines for Practice #1:

본인이 작성한 에세이에(아직 혹시 안 했으면 지금 50분간 꼭 작성해 본 후 이 설명을 볼 것!) 다음의 요소들이 정확히, 또 예와 함께 완전하게 작성되었는지 확인해 볼 것이다. 미처 분석하지 못하거나 실수한 부분이 있다면 다시 작성하면서 실력을 improve 할 수 있도록 복습할 것!

"The Selfish Side of Gratitude" by Barbara Ehrenreich

일단 이 글의 핵심은 "In the article "The Selfish Side of Gratitude," Barbara Ehrenreich asserts that, in practice, gratitude has evolved into a rather selfish act"라고 기술하면 적절하겠다.

분석에 있어서는 다음의 세 부분 관련하여 각각 적절한 내용이 있어야 한다:

1. Evidences – Ehrenreich's approach was the use of citing authorities and celebrities, in an interesting and unconventional way of introducing the prevalence of the 'antithesis' that is to be disputed in this article. (주의할 점은 글쓴이 자신의 주장을 위해서가 아닌 반박하는 의견이 얼마나 사회에 만연해 있는가를 보여 주기 위해 이렇게 했다는 점이다.) + Ehrenreich also employs the use of concrete examples as a way of conveying her points.

2. Reasoning – there is deep analytical reasoning found in the author's delivery of the argument. + Moral reasoning about what is not so right about the practice (원래 'you and him/her'가 되어야 하는데 'you and you'라고 지적하고 있다) + the 'hypocrisy' of the Templeton foundation.

3. Styles – there is the use of vivid and delicate languages. + Allusion by using the 'NY Times reader' as a member of a privileged class.

SAT-Essay-Practice Test #2:

> Analyze and write about the following passage, following the instructions given at the end (50 minutes):
>
> The reading passage is taken from Richard Schiffman, "Working less would provide much to Americans" The Washington Post (January 27, 2012.)
>
> * *Retrieved online through:*
>   *https://www.washingtonpost.com/opinions/working-less-would-provide-much-to-americans/2012/01/26/gIQArhKPWQ_story.html?noredirect=on&utm_term=.9b63c1aa7136*

1.
Recently a friend confided over dinner that her job was "killing" her. I was surprised. She is a director of a midsize nonprofit that is doing citizen diplomacy work in the Middle East, and she has often remarked on how gratifying it is to be involved in a program that brings historical enemies face to face to share their stories.

2.
But 2011 was a tough year for fundraisers, and my friend has been doing double duty as her understaffed organization struggles to make up the shortfall. Like many nowadays, she takes her work home with her, which

has taken a toll on her personal life, health and sleep. She is thinking of leaving the nonprofit but is afraid to do so before she finds another job.

3.
Another friend who is employed by a large insurance company is routinely forced to work late and at home on weekends — often without pay — on the projects she didn't have time to finish at the office. With the threat of layoffs ever-present, she dares not complain about this modern-day slave labor.

4.
Americans already work hundreds of hours a year more than their counterparts in other developed countries, including workaholic Japan. They also have fewer days off than Europeans, who typically take four to six weeks of paid vacation a year.

5.
Companies argue that grueling work schedules are necessary to boost productivity. But consider that, despite the recession, the productivity of U.S. workers has increased fourfold since the 1950s. Put another way, as of 2000, employees work one hour to produce what it took four hours to create a half-century ago. Meanwhile, the buying power of wages has remained stagnant and in recent years has even begun to decline. Someone is getting rich off the exponential rise in productivity, but it is not the American worker.

6.
In the past, unions struggled not only to raise pay but also to shorten the hours that their members had to work. The trend toward shorter hours

continued unabated from the Civil War through the end of the Great Depression and the enactment, in 1938, of the Fair Labor Standard Act's 40-hour-week provision. But during World War II work hours increased sharply, and it has not been a significant public issue since.

7.
Given the recent troubles in the U.S. economy, this may seem an odd moment to reconsider the value of working less. But this crisis is not due to poor productivity; U.S. workers' productivity is at an all-time high. Neither is it a crisis in corporate profitability, which continues to soar despite tough economic times for ordinary Americans. It is arguably a crisis in corporate greed, one created by financial entities pushing for ever higher growth rates and levels of profitability regardless of the cost to the long-term health of the economy or for those whose hard work made that economy flourish over the past century.

8.
Americans know that we can no longer afford a corporate culture on steroids that generates unsustainable profits by systematically cannibalizing our nation and the people who make it work. So a good place to start applying the brakes on this runaway train would be making sure that we don't have to kill ourselves at work just to make a living.

9.
A wide-scale reduction in work hours would spread out the national workload and help to make more jobs available for the unemployed. Historically, shorter workweeks have been as large a creator of new jobs as market growth, sociology professor Juliet Schor argued last year.

10.

While shorter hours would mean less income for many, nearly half of Americans surveyed in 2004 by the Center for a New American Dream said that they would be willing to accept a smaller paycheck in return for more time with their families and leisure. This would help explain the popularity of four-day workweeks; a pilot program in Utah found 82 percent of state workers surveyed said that they liked the change and wanted to stick with it.

11.

The benefits of shortening the workweek would be incalculable for Americans' health and well being. And it would even be good for the planet. A 2006 study by the Center for Economic and Policy Research estimated that, if the United States were to emulate the shorter workweeks of Western Europe, energy consumption would decline about 20 percent and our country could significantly diminish its carbon footprint. Millions of Americans could live with less stress and more happiness and fulfillment.

12.

With so much to gain, we need to cut work hours while there is still time.

> **Instruction**
>
> *Write an essay in which you explain how* Richard Schiffman *builds the argument. In your essay, analyze how the author uses one or more of the features of evidences, reasoning, and styles (or features of your own choice) to strengthen the logic and persuasiveness of his argument. Be sure that your analysis focuses on the most relevant aspects of the passage.*
>
> *Your essay should not explain whether you agree with the author's claims, but rather explain how the author builds an argument to persuade his audience.*

*트레이닝 Guidelines for Practice #2:

여기서도 본인이 작성한 에세이에 다음의 요소들이 적절히 반영되어 있는지 확인해 볼 것이다. 그리고 다시 작성하면서 실력을 키우는 re-writing을 할 것!

"Working less would provide much to Americans" by Richard Schiffman

일단 이 글의 핵심은 "Richard Schiffman successfully delivered a clear and convincing message to his readers with respect to the benefits of reducing work hours for Americans"라고 기술하면 되겠다.

분석에 있어서는 다음의 세 부분 관련하여 각각 적절한 내용이 있어야 한다:

1. **Evidences** – Richard Schiffman's approaches are through offering statistical data and referring to authorities regarding the benefits of reducing work hours for Americans.
2. **Reasoning** – the author mainly chose to point out the flaws in the counterarguments followed by the explanations on the benefits of working less (consequential reasoning).
3. **Styles** – these aspects are intertwined with the author's skillful adoption of metaphors as the main stylistic element of his essay.

SAT-Essay-Practice Test #3:

Analyze and write about the following passage, following the instructions given at the end (50 minutes):

The reading passage is taken from Robert Redford: "Protect Our Wild Horses", published in USA Today, November 3, 2014.

* Retrieved online through:
  https://www.usatoday.com/story/opinion/2014/11/03/wild-horses-rancers-federal-government-standoff/18060665/

1.
Horses and I have had a shared existence, personal and professional, for as long as I can remember. And while I carry a strong passion for all horses, my tenacious support for the preservation of habitat for wildlife and the American mustangs derives from their symbolic representation of our national heritage and freedom.

2.
Any infringement on their legally protected right to live freely is an assault on America's principles. The varied and subjective interpretation of laws intended to protect these animals on our public lands, continues to leave wild horses under attack.

3.
Recent "stand-offs" between ranchers and the federal government are reminiscent of old westerns. But this American tragedy does not have a hero riding in to save the day, and wild horses have become the victim in the controversies over our public land resources.

4.
In 1971, as a result of concern for America's dwindling wild horse populations, the US Congress passed the Wild Free Roaming Horse and Burro Act. . The Act mandated that the Bureau of Land Management (BLM), protect free roaming wild horses and burros, under a multiple use management policy, on designated areas of our public lands.

5.
The BLM manages 245 million acres of our public lands, with livestock grazing permits on 155 million acres. Wild horses are designated to share a mere 26.9 million acres. That means only 17% of BLM-managed public land are made available to wild horses. Wild horse populations vary between 32,000 and 50,000 while livestock grazing allocations accommodate numbers in the millions. Yes, in the millions.

6.
Advocates are only asking that the horses be treated fairly. Wild horses are consistently targeted as the primary cause of negative impact to grazing lands resulting from decades of propaganda that ignores math, science and solutions that can be implemented today.

7.

Ranchers hold nearly 18,000 grazing lease permits on BLM land alone. Grazing costs on BLM land goes for $1.35 per cow and calf pair, well below the market rate of $16. This price disparity derived from BLM's current permit policy establishes an uneven playing field on grazing economies. Understandably ranchers have a vested interest in maintaining the status quo.

8.

Although less than 3% of America's beef is produced on federal land, this subsidized grazing program costs the taxpayer more than $123 million dollars a year, and more than $500 million when indirect costs are accounted for.

9.

The long-term economic success of public lands lies in maintaining a bio diverse ecosystem within its boundaries. However, understanding the need for a preservation balance in thriving agricultural communities often becomes sidelined.

10.

The BLM needs to comply with its original "multiple use" principle in managing wild horses and burros. In light of the inequitable share of livestock on BLM land, the on going persecution of wild horses and those that value them is unacceptable and threatens the very spirit of the American West. I urge Congress to stand up for much needed reform of the BLM's wild horse and burro program and livestock grazing on federal lands.

11.

Now is not the time to repudiate environmental balance, but rather it is the time for all of us to work together – politician, advocate, rancher, scientist, and citizen. Only by doing this will the United States move forward and be a leader in environmental issues and ensure sustainability to our delicate ecosystem.

> [Instruction]
>
> *Write an essay in which you explain how* Robert Redford *builds the argument. In your essay, analyze how the author uses one or more of the features of evidences, reasoning, and styles (or features of your own choice) to strengthen the logic and persuasiveness of his argument. Be sure that your analysis focuses on the most relevant aspects of the passage.*
>
> *Your essay should not explain whether you agree with the author's claims, but rather explain how the author builds an argument to persuade his audience.*

∗ 트레이닝 Guidelines for Practice #3:

앞서와 같이 본인이 작성한 에세이에 다음의 요소들이 적절히 반영되어 있는지 확인해 본 후 다시 작성하면서 실력을 키우는 복습을 할 것!

"Protect Our Wild Horses" by Robert Redford

이 글의 핵심은 "Writing in reaction to the conditions of endangered wild horses, Redford adamantly argues that people should do more to protect the horses"라고 하면 적절하겠다.

분석에 있어서는 다음의 세 부분 관련하여 각각 적절한 내용이 있어야 한다:

1. Evidences – Redford starts his argument off by employing his personal anecdote; Redford points out directly that the reason for his writing the article [are] the "shared", "personal", and "professional" encounters…
2. Reasoning – the author mainly resorts to moral reasoning, with some consequential reasoning about what is in the best interests for Americans in the long run (appeal to self-interest).
3. Styles – these aspects are intertwined with the author's use of striking, potent contrasts.

SAT-Essay-Practice Test #4:

> Analyze and write about the following passage, following the instructions at the end (50 minutes):
>
> The reading passage is taken from Frank Bruni, "Read, Kids, Read". ©2014 by New York Times.
>
> * *Retrieved online through:*
>   *https://www.nytimes.com/2014/05/13/opinion/bruni-read-kids-read.html*

1.
As an uncle I'm inconsistent about too many things. Birthdays, for example. My nephew Mark had one on Sunday, and I didn't remember — and send a text — until 10 p.m., by which point he was asleep.
School productions, too. I saw my niece Bella in "Seussical: The Musical" but missed "The Wiz." She played Toto, a feat of trans-species transmogrification that not even Meryl, with all of her accents, has pulled off.

2.
But about books, I'm steady. Relentless. I'm incessantly asking my nephews and nieces what they're reading and why they're not reading more. I'm reliably hurling novels at them, and also at friends' kids. I may well be responsible for 10 percent of all sales of "The Fault in Our Stars," a teenage love story to be released as a movie next month. Never have I

spent money with fewer regrets, because I believe in reading — not just in its power to transport but in its power to transform.

3.

So I was crestfallen on Monday, when a new report by Common Sense Media came out. It showed that 30 years ago, only 8 percent of 13-year-olds and 9 percent of 17-year-olds said that they "hardly ever" or never read for pleasure. Today, 22 percent of 13-year-olds and 27 percent of 17-year-olds say that. Fewer than 20 percent of 17-year-olds now read for pleasure "almost every day." Back in 1984, 31 percent did. What a marked and depressing change.

4.

I know, this sounds like a fogy's crotchety lament*. Or, worse, like self-interest. Professional writers arguing for vigorous reading are dinosaurs begging for a last breath. We're panhandlers with a better vocabulary. But I'm coming at this differently, as someone persuaded that reading does things — to the brain, heart and spirit — that movies, television, video games and the rest of it cannot. There's research on this, and it's cited in a recent article in The Guardian by Dan Hurley, who wrote that after "three years interviewing psychologists and neuroscientists around the world," he'd concluded that "reading and intelligence have a relationship so close as to be symbiotic."

5.

In terms of smarts and success, is reading causative or merely correlated? Which comes first, "The Hardy Boys" or the hardy mind? That's difficult to unravel, but several studies have suggested that people who read fiction, reveling in its analysis of character and motivation, are more adept at reading people, too: at sizing up the social whirl around them.

They're more empathetic. God knows we need that.
Late last year, neuroscientists at Emory University reported enhanced neural activity in people who'd been given a regular course of daily reading, which seemed to jog the brain: to raise its game, if you will.

6.

Some experts have doubts about that experiment's methodology, but I'm struck by how its findings track something that my friends and I often discuss. If we spend our last hours or minutes of the night reading rather than watching television, we wake the next morning with thoughts less jumbled, moods less jangled. Reading has bequeathed what meditation promises. It has smoothed and focused us.

7.

Maybe that's about the quiet of reading, the pace of it. At Success Academy Charter Schools in New York City, whose students significantly outperform most peers statewide, the youngest kids all learn and play chess, in part because it hones "the ability to focus and concentrate," said Sean O'Hanlon, who supervises the program. Doesn't reading do the same?

8.

Daniel Willingham, a psychology professor at the University of Virginia, framed it as a potentially crucial corrective to the rapid metabolism and sensory overload of digital technology. He told me that it can demonstrate to kids that there's payoff in "doing something taxing, in delayed gratification." A new book of his, "Raising Kids Who Read," will be published later this year.

9.

Before talking with him, I arranged a conference call with David Levithan and Amanda Maciel. Both have written fiction in the young adult genre, whose current robustness is cause to rejoice, and they rightly noted that the intensity of the connection that a person feels to a favorite novel, with which he or she spends eight or 10 or 20 hours, is unlike any response to a movie.

10.

That observation brought to mind a moment in "The Fault in Our Stars" when one of the protagonists says that sometimes, "You read a book and it fills you with this weird evangelical zeal, and you become convinced that the shattered world will never be put back together unless and until all living humans read the book." Books are personal, passionate. They stir emotions and spark thoughts in a manner all their own, and I'm convinced that the shattered world has less hope for repair if reading becomes an ever smaller part of it.

* = whimsical, ill-tempered complaint that does not seem to make any sense

Instruction

Write an essay in which you explain how Frank Bruni builds the argument. In your essay, analyze how the author uses one or more of the features of evidences, reasoning, and styles (or features of your own choice) to strengthen the logic and persuasiveness of his argument. Be sure that your analysis focuses on the most relevant aspects of the passage.

Your essay should not explain whether you agree with the author's claims, but rather explain how the author builds an argument to persuade his audience.

* 트레이닝 Guidelines for Practice #4:

여기서도 본인이 작성한 에세이에 다음의 요소들이 적절히 반영되어 있는지 확인해 본 후 다시 작성하면서 실력을 키우는 복습을 할 것! (한 번 이해하고 지나치면 실력이나 감각은 좋아지더라도 실전에서 더 잘할 수 있다는 보장은 없다. - 다시 쓰면서 확실히 실력이 느는 것이다.)

"Read, Kids, Read" by Frank Bruni

이 글의 핵심은 "Frank Bruni successfully delivered a clear and convincing message to his readers with respect to the benefits of reading for children" 라고 하면 적절하겠다.

분석에 있어서는 다음의 세 부분 관련하여 각각 적절한 내용이 있어야 한다:

1. Evidences - Bruni's attempts to offer statistical data and references to authorities regarding the benefits of reading for children boosted the logical quality of his message.
2. Reasoning - the author mainly resorts to embracing counterarguments, and then refuting them (+ consequential reasoning about the benefits of reading for children).
3. Styles - these aspects are intertwined with the author's introduction use of personal anecdotes and first-person perspectives.

SAT-Essay-Practice Test #5:

> Analyze and write about the following passage, following the instructions given at the end (50 minutes):
>
> The reading passage is taken from Patrick T. Harker, "Student Athletes Shouldn't Unionize" ©2014 by The New York Times Company. Published on April 1, 2014.
>
> * Retrieved online through:
>   https://www.nytimes.com/2014/04/02/opinion/student-athletes-shouldnt-unionize.html

1.

Last week's ruling by a regional director of the National Labor Relations Board that players on Northwestern University's football team were school employees, and thus eligible to unionize, has been celebrated by those who believe that it will benefit student athletes everywhere.

2.

It won't. Player unions would be a disaster for universities, for college sports fans and, most important, for student athletes themselves. The prospect of college football players bargaining to exchange scholarships for salaries is still remote, but if it comes about, even the most valuable athletes would be worse off.

3.
Turning student athletes into salaried employees would endanger the existence of varsity sports on many college campuses. Only about 10 percent of Division I college sports programs turn a profit, and most of them, like our $28 million athletic program at the University of Delaware, lose money. Changing scholarship dollars into salary would almost certainly increase the amount schools have to spend on sports, since earnings are taxed and scholarships are not. In order just to match the value of a scholarship, the university would have to spend more.

4.
We are among the many schools that have already had to trim varsity sports in recent years. Should costs increase, we and many other schools would face pressure to cut back further.

5.
Without question, some big schools have lost their way. On some campuses the pursuit of athletic dominance has eroded the ideal of the student athlete. Players at these schools have every right to complain, particularly when the demands of competition effectively prevent them from being students. But the answer is not to organize and essentially turn pro. This would only further lessen the priority on learning. If scholarship athletes already find it hard to balance schoolwork with team commitments, under arrangements that obligate educational opportunity, think how much harder it would be if they were being paid to play.

6.
The answer for young athletes who want to be paid to play is not to target universities, which have a different mission, but professional sports leagues like the National Basketball Association and the National Football League, which still bar high school athletes from turning pro. If players

are good enough to earn a living at that age, I say, let them. Very few, however, are that good. At the college level, even the highest-ranked teams field relatively few players who will ever play a day of professional sports.

7.
Strong athletic departments do two things well. They afford young athletes the chance to reach their full potential, and they prepare them for life when the cheering stops. For the vast majority of student athletes, that life begins at graduation. For the exceptional ones who make it to the pros, post-sport life begins soon enough. The average length of a pro football career is only about three years.

8.
Valuing education doesn't have to compromise an athlete's potential. Here at the University of Delaware, Elena Delle Donne played women's basketball from 2009 to 2013, earning top collegiate honors and helping the team become one of the best in the nation. She was a top pick in the Women's National Basketball Association draft and was later named rookie of the year. In college, she maintained a 3.6 G.P.A., earning a degree in human services.

9.
My own experience as a student athlete was more typical. I was a good student in high school, and a good football player. My options at graduation were greatly multiplied by my success as an athlete. I accepted financial help to play at the University of Pennsylvania, where I majored in engineering. An injury in my junior year brought my football career to an end. Then I discovered my passion for research, went on to earn a Ph.D. in engineering and embarked on a path that has taken me places I never imagined when playing on a defensive line.

10.
This is the reality for most college athletes, even in the five major conferences. If the football players at Northwestern think they will do better for themselves by collecting a salary in college, they're wrong.

11.
My advice, even to those talented enough to turn pro straight out of high school, is the same: Play ball but be smart. Earn a degree.

> **Instruction**
>
> *Write an essay in which you explain how* Patrick Harker *builds the argument. In your essay, analyze how the author uses one or more of the features of evidences, reasoning, and styles (or features of your own choice) to strengthen the logic and persuasiveness of his argument. Be sure that your analysis focuses on the most relevant aspects of the passage.*
>
> *Your essay should not explain whether you agree with the author's claims, but rather explain how the author builds an argument to persuade his audience.*

* 트레이닝 Guidelines for Practice #5:

다시 한번 본인이 작성한 에세이에 다음의 요소들이 적절히 반영되어 있는지 밑의 사항을 참조하여 확인해 본 후 다시 작성하면서 실력을 키우는 복습을 할 것!

"Student Athletes Shouldn't Unionize" by Patrick T. Harker

이 글의 핵심은 "Patrick T. Harker writes this article in the NY Times in an attempt to persuade the readers that student athletes' unions should not be allowed"라고 소스를 살짝 언급하면서 기술해 보아도 적절하겠다.

분석에 있어서는 다음의 세 부분 관련하여 각각 적절한 내용이 작성되어야 한다:

1. Evidences – Harker's main strategy is the use of statistical data and a concrete case.
2. Reasoning – the author turns to deep analytical reasoning about the consequences that can be anticipated, combined with moral reasoning about what is the right thing to do, to strengthen the trustworthiness of his argument.
3. Styles – the author adds a personal anecdote as the main stylistic element to his essay.

SAT-Essay-Practice Test #6:

> Analyze and write about the following passage, following the instructions given at the end (50 minutes):
>
> The reading passage is taken from the former President Lyndon B. Johnson's "The Voting Rights Address", delivered to the American public on March 15, 1965.
>
> * *Retrieved online through:*
>   *http://law.jrank.org/pages/11765/Lyndon-B-Johnson-Voting-Rights-Act-Address-Lyndon-B-Johnson-Voting-Rights-Act-Address.html*

1.
I speak tonight for the dignity of man and the destiny of democracy.

2.
I urge every member of both parties—Americans of all religions and of all colors—from every section of this country—to join me in that cause.

3.
At times history and fate meet at a single time in a single place to shape a turning point in man's unending search for freedom. So it was at Lexington and Concord. So it was a century ago at Appomattox. So it was last week in Selma, Alabama.

4.

There is no Negro problem. There is no southern problem. There is no northern problem. There is only an American problem. And we are met here tonight as Americans—not as Democrats or Republicans—we are met here as Americans to solve that problem.

5.

This was the first nation in the history of the world to be founded with a purpose. The great phrases of that purpose still sound in every American heart, north and south: "All men are created equal"—"Government by consent of the governed"—"Give me liberty or give me death."…

6.

Those words are a promise to every citizen that he shall share in the dignity of man. This dignity cannot be found in man's possessions. It cannot be found in his power or in his position. It really rests on his right to be treated as a man equal in opportunity to all others. It says that he shall share in freedom, he shall choose his leaders, educate his children, provide for his family according to his ability and his merits as a human being….

7.

Many of the issues of civil rights are very complex and most difficult. But about this there can and should be no argument. Every American citizen must have an equal right to vote. There is no reason which can excuse the denial of that right. There is no duty which weighs more heavily on us than the duty we have to ensure that right.

8.

Yet the harsh fact is that in many places in this country men and women are kept from voting simply because they are Negroes… Experience has clearly shown that the existing process of law cannot overcome systematic and ingenious discrimination. No law that we now have on the books— and I have helped to put three of them there—can ensure the right to vote when local officials are determined to deny it.

9.

In such a case our duty must be clear to all of us. The Constitution says that no person shall be kept from voting because of his race or his color. We have all sworn an oath before God to support and to defend that Constitution. We must now act in obedience to that oath.

10.

There is no constitutional issue here. The command of the Constitution is plain. There is no moral issue. It is wrong—deadly wrong—to deny any of your fellow Americans the right to vote in this country. There is no issue of States rights or National rights. There is only the struggle for human rights.

11.

I have not the slightest doubt what will be your answer… But even if we pass this bill, the battle will not be over. What happened in Selma is part of a far larger movement which reaches into every section and State of America. It is the effort of American Negroes to secure for themselves the full blessings of American life. Their cause must be our cause too, because it is not just Negroes but really it is all of us, who must overcome the crippling legacy of bigotry and injustice. And we shall overcome….

12.
This great, rich, restless country can offer opportunity and education and hope to all—all black and white, all North and South, sharecropper and city dweller. These are the enemies—poverty, ignorance, disease—they are our enemies, not our fellow man, not our neighbor. And these enemies too—poverty, disease, and ignorance—we shall overcome.

> **Instruction**
>
> *Write an essay in which you explain how* Lyndon Johnson *builds the argument. In your essay, analyze how the author uses one or more of the features of evidences, reasoning, and styles (or features of your own choice) to strengthen the logic and persuasiveness of his argument. Be sure that your analysis focuses on the most relevant aspects of the passage.*
>
> *Your essay should* not explain whether you agree *with the author's claims, but* rather explain how the author builds an argument to *persuade his audience.*

* 트레이닝 Guidelines for Practice #6:

이제 마지막으로 정말 실전 시험이라고 마음을 굳게 다진 후 에세이를 작성해 보자! 그리고 나서 작성한 에세이에 다음의 요소들이 적절히 반영되어 있는지 밑의 사항을 참조하여 마치 본인이 채점관이 되었다고 상상하며 확인한 후, 다시 작성하면서 실력을 키우는 복습을 할 것. (+ Reading passage도 RC실력을 키울 겸 다시 한번 정독을 할 것을 권한다. - SAT 시험의 특성상 Reading과 Essay 부분의 공부가 상호 밀접한 도움이 되는 것이다!)

"The Voting Rights Address" by Lyndon B. Johnson

이 글의 핵심은 "The former president Lyndon B. Johnson delivered a powerful speech in which a clear and emotional message about the wrongfulness of denying the right to vote for African-Americans was delivered"라고 기술하면 적절하다.

분석에 있어서는 다음의 세 부분 관련하여 각각 적절한 내용이 작성되어야 한다:

1. Evidences - Johnson's main strategy is the use of concrete cases to increase the credibility of his thesis on the equal opportunities and thus voting rights for African-Americans.
2. Reasoning - Johnson mainly turns to moral reasoning, while embracing some counter-arguments and indicating its flaws.
3. Styles - the former president uses inclusive language throughout the speech to increase the emotionally appealing aspect of his speech + uses

hyperbole (과장법) and repetitions to further strengthen the emotional appeal of his speech.

(이 경우 지문이 Historical speech였기 때문에 기술할 때 동사를 전부 과거형으로 써도 적절하겠다.)

EPILOGUE

자, 이제 여기까지 SAT-Essay 트레이닝을 마쳤으면 여러분은 시험에서 고득점을 얻을 수 있는 실력의 기반을 다진 셈이다.

일단 막연히 어렵다고 생각되었던 'new' SAT-Essay 부분이 실제로는 일반적 논술형 에세이보다 오히려 쉽다는 것을 깨달았을 것이다. 이에 기초하여 자신감을 갖고 체계적 준비를 할 수 있다면 그것 자체가 성공이라 할 수 있다.

꾸준히 독해 능력을 키우고, 복습을 통하여 여기서 전수된 know-how를 완벽히 마스터한다면 반드시 목표 점수를 얻을 수 있을 것이다.
다른 요소들과 함께 대학 입시에 대비한 성공적인 준비를 하여 여러분들이 dream school로 마음에 두고 있는 학교에 합격하는 기쁨과 영광을 누리기 바란다.

Best wishes, everyone!

Appendix

A. "A Crash Course in SAT-Essay!"
   (하루 또는 이틀밖에 준비 기간이 없을 경우 응급 처방식 준비!)

B. Reasoning Pattern / Logical Thinking
   에 대한 정리

C. TOEFL Speaking & Writing Tips + Samples
   (토플 고득점 성취를 위한 스피킹 및 라이팅 트레이너 Tips!)

D. 연습용 답안지(복사용)

Appendix A

"A Crash Course in SAT-Essay!"

만약 SAT essay를 준비할 시간이 단 며칠밖에 안 되는 emergency situation에 처한 경우라면, 일단 여기 있는 극히 단순화된 접근 방식을 써서 준비해 볼 수 있다.
Full approach에 비하여 높은 점수를 기대하기는 힘들지만, 그래도 5-5-6 또는 6-5-6 정도의 'decent score'를 받을 수는 있는 방식이니 상황이 여의치 않다면 활용하기 바란다!

다음의 3 Steps를 실전 시험에 적용할 준비를 하는 것이다:

1. 일단 많이 써야 한다. – <u>최소 2페이지를 작성</u>할 준비를 하라. 힘들면 그냥 지문에 나온 것을 옮겨 적어도 된다. – 이는 분석형 에세이의 특성상 문제될 것이 없는 것이다. (다만 옮겨 적을 경우 철저하게 인용("quote")을 해야 한다는 것을 명심하라.)

2. 일단 전체 지문을 잘 읽고 <u>어떤 argument인지를 intro와 conclusion 부분에 똑같이 쓸</u> 준비를 한다. 그리고 나서 분석에 있어서는 다음 <u>두 가지 요소에 대하여만</u> 지문에 있는지 확인한 후 쓸 준비를 하라. (가장 어려운 Reasoning 부분을 과감하게 생략하고 'Evidences'와 'Styles' 두 부분에 대하여서만 분석하여 쓰는 것이다.

A. Evidences - 전략적 요소:

- Use of statistics: 각종 통계적 사실을 인용하는 경우
- Citing case studies: 잘 알려진 또는 학술적으로 연구된 사례를 인용하는 경우
- Reference to authorities: 권위가 있는 전문가나 지도자, 또는 기관의 의견이나 주장을 언급하는 경우

B. Stylistic elements - 스타일적인 요소:

- Personal anecdotes + first person language / perspectives: 개인적 일화 소개 및 1인칭 관점의 언어 사용
- Contrasts / parallelism / repetitions: 대조, 병치, 반복 등을 통하여 강조 효과를 내는 방법
- Similes / metaphors / allusions (implications) / synecdoche: 직유나 은유법 등을 통하여 효과적인 이미지나 감성을 전달하는 방법
- Hyperbole / vivid language: 과장법이나 생생한 표현으로 기술하는 부분
- Rhetorical questions: 수사적 질문을 던져 독자의 경각심을 일으키는 방법

3. 위에 언급된 A와 B 각 분야에서 하나 또는 두 개의 주요 포인트를 아웃라인 list 형식으로 간단히 메모한 후 Template을 사용하여 작성한다. 미리 철저히 format을 준비하여 작성 과정에서 여러 부분에 대하여 어떤 표현을 쓸 것인가에 대한 고민을 하지 않도록 한다. 본인만의 준비된 것이 있으면 그걸 다시 상기하여 쓸 준비를 하고 그렇지 않다면 다음의 Template을 쓰라. ('examples'로 표시된 부분에는 지문의 해당 내용을 옮겨 적으면 되는 것이다.)

The topic of the article by (author) is (the topic) which is an important issue for our society. In presenting his/her argument to the readers / audience, the author relied on ──────, ──────, and ────────, ensuring the persuasiveness in his/her argument.

When the evidences in the passage are examined, the author's strategy in presenting argument is the use of _____. *(+ Examples)*
Then, (the author) also uses_____. *(+ Examples)*

+ These strategies render his/her argument logically very strong.

Furthermore, when it comes to the stylistic elements, the author uses _____. *(+ Examples)*

Also, _____ is also adopted in the author's writing. *(+ Examples)*

+ These stylistic components increases the level of emotional appeal of his/her message to the readers / audience.

(The author)'s argument is elaborately and skillfully constructed with ———, ———, and ———. By utilizing these components in his/her argument, the author successfully delivered a clear and convincing message to the readers / audience.

이 템플릿은 완전히 암기하여 실전에서 기억이 나지 않아 우왕좌왕하는 일이 없도록 한다.

자, 이렇게 위의 3 Step을 준비하면 *decent score*는 받을 수 있는 최소한의 준비는 되는 것이다!

Good luck!

Appendix B
Reasoning Pattern / Logical Thinking에 대한 정리

이 부분에서는 Reasoning patterns - logical rules of thinking에 대하여 정리가 되어 있다. 필자가 다년간 argumentative essay나 college application essays를 지도해 오면서 발전시킨 설득력 제고를 위한 효율적 논리적 틀인 것이다.

7개의 '논리적 생각의 틀'을 염두에 두고 글을 분석하거나 자신의 의견을 생성하는 데 활용하면 효과적으로 reasoning을 알아볼 수 있고, 또 조리 있고 설득력 있는 생각을 만들어 낼 수 있을 것이다.

Rule #1

> The practice of thinking about everything in terms of three distinctive aspects: **practical, psychological, and social!**

사회 현상의 다양한 변수를 이 세 가지 측면으로 분류하여 접근하는 논리의 기본 틀이다. 모든 주제에 대하여 실질적 또는 현실적(practical / realistic or sometimes physical), 심리적(psychological / emotional), 그리고 사회적(social /

interpersonal or related to the society as a whole or sometimes 'international') 인 면을 생각해 보고, 또 그에 대한 답도 그 세 방향에서 제시해 보는 Reasoning 방식인 것이다. 많은 경우 장단점 또는 예상되는 혜택이나 손실 등을 이러한 분야별로 설명하는 경우가 주장의 근거로 쓰일 수 있는 것이다. 특히 여러 사회 현상의 원인에 대한 생각이 필요할 때 이 방식을 쓰면 조리 있게 구성된 outline을 얻는 것이 수월해진다. (때로는 문맥에 따라 이러한 사항들이 'basic human nature'라고 주장될 수도 있다.)

이 방식은 논리적으로 자신의 주장을 펴는 데 있어 가장 기본적으로 쓰일 수 있는 유용한 방법으로, 설득력 있는 주장의 기반이 되는 포인트를 내용상 중복됨이 없이 생각하여 낼 수 있도록 도와주는 'fundamental framework / template of thinking'이라고 할 수 있다. (By the way, this is referred to as 'Steven's framework!')

Rule #2

> Think about the currently dominant conditions around the world, and go with those conditions – There are usually good reasons why the things are the way they are!

우리 사회의 현 상황을 의견의 찬반 여부를 가리는 기반으로 삼는 논리적 틀이다! 일반적으로 보면 사회의 현 상황은 그에 타당한 이유가 있어서 형성되고 유지되는 경우가 대부분이다. 예를 들어 "부모 면허제를 실시한다"든가, "의무 투표제"를 도입해야 한다'는 의견에 대하여 뚜렷한 방향이 잡히지 않으면, '현재 우리 사회가 그러한 제도나 법안을 가지고 있는가?'라는 물음을 던져 답을 구한 후 그에 기초하여 설득력 있는 argument를 펴는 경우이다. 두 경우 모두 한국 사회에서 실시하지 않고 있는데, 그 이유는 개인의 자유의지에 대한 불필요한 간섭이나 사생활 침해 등의 소지가 있고, 법의 집행 과정에 있어서도 많은 현실적 어려움이 있기 때문이다. 아마도 제안된 적이 있어도 시행되고 있지 않을 텐데, 그러한 이유를 기본 근거로 논리를 발전시키면 설득력 있는 argument를 제시할 수 있다.

Rule #3

> "More is better, and new is better, holding other variables constant!"
> (Those are often the more 'advanced,' and thus 'better' conditions, with exceptions, of course.)

다른 변수들이 동일하다고 가정하였을 때 일단 많은 것이 좋고, 새로운 것이 좋은 선택이라는 생각의 틀이다! 이는 더 많은 면을 가지거나, 더 최근에 나온 생각이나 방식이 일반적으로 더 많은 혜택이나 이점을 포함하는 경우가 많고, 그리하여 더 진일보한 선택인 경우가 빈번하다는 논리에 기초하는 생각이다.

이 룰이 적용되는 경우의 예를 들면, '세계화를 통한 Multiculturalism이 과거의 전통 문화를 고수하는 것보다는 더 윤택한 문화생활을 할 수 있게 하므로 더 낫다'는 견해, '도서관이 앞으로 계속 e-books / e-storage를 활용하는 방향으로 나아가는 것이 좋다'는 입장, '과거의 권위적 정부보다는 liberal democracy가 장기적으로 보면 국민들의 변화하는 요구에 더 융통성 있게 반응할 수 있고, 혁신적인 기업 마인드 등을 촉진할 수 있다는 점 등으로 보아 더 나은 perspective이다'라고 주장을 펴는 경우 등이 있겠다.

Rule #4

> When an idea can obviously be approached from both the pro and con sides, take the middle road, and make an argument that it <u>'depends' on some other variables!</u> (+ Remember, "extreme" is usually bad!)

주제의 성격상 타당성이나 찬반 여부가 관련된 상황이나 조건에 따라 완전히 달라질 수 있는 경우가 있을 수 있다는 Reasoning이 있다. 이러한 생각의 틀은 특히 어떠한 법률 또는 정책의 시행이 성공적으로 이루어지려면 필요한 선행 조건이 무엇이겠는가라는 종류의 문제에 대응할 때 많이 쓰인다. 예를 들어 'Increasing the price of gasoline is an effective way to reduce the number of people driving their private vehicles'라는 주제가 있다면, "It is not so simple; the effectiveness of such a policy would depend on the current level of the gasoline price in the given society, and the profiles of the users of private vehicles, too"라고 반응하는 경우이다. 해당 지역에서의 현재 휘발유 가격대가 얼마인지, 그리고 주로 어떤 목적으로 개인 차량들이 사용되고 있는가에 따라 그 정책의 효과가 결정될 것이기 때문이다. + 추가로 <u>"extreme is undesirable" – 과하면 독이 된다는 논리도 기억할 것!</u> 의견이 extreme하게 느껴지는 경우가 있는데, '뭐든지 과하면 좋지 않다'는 생각을 가지고 접근하면 그에 대한 논리적인 의견을 피력할 수 있다. 예를 들어, "요즘 젊은이들은 모두 강남 스타일을 좋아한다"라는 말을 평가하자면 '모두'란 부분을 문제 삼아 과한 표현으로 논리적이지 못하다고 지적하면 된다. 그리고 나서 의견을 develop할 때는 예외의 경우를 생각해 내면 된다. (Think about possible exceptions!)

Rule #5

> **Think about the basic governing rules of our society, especially the democratic and capitalistic principles, when organizing your thoughts!**

민주주의나 자본주의의 원칙을 염두에 두고 어떤 생각이나 주장이 '맞는지'를 주장할 수 있다. 때로는 역사적, 사회적 사실에 근거해서 판단하거나 또는 '인본주의적 원칙'(humanitarian principles)을 잣대로 삼을 수도 있다. 이러한 '원칙'이나 '근본적 가치'에 기초하여 주장을 펴는 것은 일종의 "Moral reasoning"이라고 할 수 있다. 자유, 평등과 같은 민주주의의 원칙과 사유재산의 인정, 수요와 공급을 통한 재화의 가치 결정 등의 자본주의의 원칙을 생각하여 의견을 결정하는 데 사용하면 유용하다. 다만 이러한 원칙들의 시행에 있어서는 ideal한 면과 realistic한 면이 다른 경우가 많으며, 또한 원칙들 간 상호 보완적이거나 반대로 상충되는 경우도 있음에 유의해야 한다.

Rule #6

> Always think about 'cause and effect' relationships, and be careful not to confuse correlations with causations. Also, remember the basic need to consider the root cause of a problem when you are trying to come up with solutions for solving the problem!

많은 경우 원인과 결과의 관계를 분석적으로 생각하여 그에 근거를 두고 어떤 주장을 펴는 경우가 있다. 특히 문화 현상이나 사회 문제의 해결책에 대한 질문이 주어졌을 경우, 기본적으로 원인을 분석하여 그것에 대한 조치를 취해야 한다는 생각의 틀에 기초한 Reasoning이 유효한 경우가 많다.

또한 연구나 관찰에 근거한 주장을 평가하는 문제가 주어지면, 상관관계(correlation)를 인과관계(causation)로 잘못 인식하지 않았는지에 대한 생각을 해야 한다. 예를 들어 과거의 심리학 논문 중 '아이스크림이 사람들로 하여금 더 공격적 성향을 가지도록 만든다'라는 주장을 펴는 것이 있었는데, 이는 뉴욕에서 진행된 간단한 연구에 기초된 것으로서 여름철 아이스크림 판매량이 늘어나면 폭력 행위로 경찰에 검거되는(arrested for aggravated assaults) 사람의 수가 증가한다라는 자료에서 근거했다. 이 논문은 사회과학 분야에서 data를 잘못 해석한 대표적 경우로 인용되곤 하는데, 아이스크림의 섭취가 원인이 되어 폭력 사건이 증가하는 것이 아니라 여름철 불쾌지수와 사람들이 외부에서 머무는 시간이 증가함에 따라 갈등 상황도 증가하여 생기는 현상이었던 것이다. 또한 사회 문제나 갈등 상황 등을 제시하고 이에 대한 해결책 또는 추구해야 할 변화의 방향을 묻는 문제에 대하여는 근본적 원인이 무엇이므로 제도 개혁이나 교육, 홍보를 통하여 그러한 요소를 최대한 줄여야 한다는 식으로 주장을 펴는 것이 논리적인 답이 된다.

Rule #7

> Be critical about the results of research findings reported by considering the representativeness of the samples used, and the logical quality of the thinking processes involved in drawing conclusions based on the obtained data!

연구 결과나 사회 현상 등에 관한 가설의 타당성에 대한 의견을 피력하는 경우, 일단 방법론적으로 적절한지 분석하여 보고, 연관된 모든 변수들이 적절히 고려되었는지, 그렇지 않다면 **단순화의 오류**(oversimplification) 또는 **과잉 일반화의 오류**(overgeneralization) 등의 문제가 없는지가 주장을 뒷받침하는 근거가 될 수 있다! (SAT-Essay의 경우는 'counter arguments'를 평가하는 데 이 reasoning이 사용될 수 있는 것이다.)

우선적으로 연구에 포함된 표본 집단이 모집단 전체를 대표하는 성격을 적절히 갖추었는지를 고려해야 한다. (ex. using the group of only the 12th grade when studying the issue of 'teenage' suicide) 또한 연구 결과를 해석하고 적용하는 과정에서 연구자가 주장하고자 하는 바에 부합되는 내용만을 선별적으로 인용하는 (selective attention) 오류가 있지 않은지 생각하여 주장에 반영할 수 있다.

(+ Additional Rule)

Think about the possible positive and negative consequences, and use them as points to support your arguments!

어떤 변화에 따른 가능한 결과를 생각하여 그 변화가 바람직한지 아닌지를 주장하는 논리의 근거가 될 수 있다! (SAT-Essay에서 이런 경우를 'consequential reasoning' 으로 기술할 수 있다.)

이 생각의 틀은 특히 다른 대안이 도저히 생각나지 않을 때 유용하게 쓰일 수 있는 사항으로, 매우 다양한 주제에 대한 논리적 대응에 쓰일 수 있다. 또한 예상되는 어떠한 혜택이 손해보다 더 많을 것이다(outweigh)라는 포인트, 또는 그 반대로 부정적 결과가 혜택을 상쇄할 것이다(offset / cancel each other out)라는 점을 논리적 근거로 하여 자신의 주장을 펼치거나 상대의 의견에 대한 타당성 있는 비판을 제시할 수 있는 것이다.

Appendix C

TOEFL Speaking & Writing Tips + Samples
(토플 고득점 성취를 위한 스피킹 및 라이팅 트레이너 Tips!)

많은 SAT 수험생들이 대학 지원 시 제출해야 하는 경우가 많은 TOEFL, 그러나 의외로 Speaking과 Writing 부분이 걸림돌이 되는 경우가 많다. 그래서 그 두 부분에 대하여 간략하게 Tip을 제시하고, 참고할 수 있는 Sample을 제공하고자 한다.

꽤 오랜 기간 TOEFL을 준비했는데도 이 두 부분에 있어 고득점을 성취하지 못했거나, 또는 해외에서 장기간 거주하여 영어 구사와 작문에는 자신이 있으나 TOEFL시험 유형에 익숙하지 않아 어려움을 겪는 경우의 학생에게 특히 도움이 될 수 있을 것이다.

TOEFL Speaking 트레이너 Tips:

1. 일단 크고 똑똑하게 말한다

평소 작고 소근소근 말하는 것이 버릇인 학생들은 특히 이 점에 유의한다. 발음 자체는 평가 요소는 아니지만, 소리의 크기와 에너지는 학생의 답변에 대한 자신감을 나타내 주는 간접적 징표이기 때문에 점수에 내용 못지않은 영향을 줄 수 있다. (말에 힘이 없는 학생들은 특히 독립형 문제의 답에서 definitely / strongly / indeed / most certainly 그리고 of course / just / exactly 등의 강조적 의미의 부사 표현을 풍부하게 사용하여 답의 'enthusiasm'이 더 느껴지게 하면 효과적이다.
e.g. "I wouldn't feel right about it." → "I just wouldn't feel right about it.")

2. 생각의 Rule을 준비해서 활용하라
이 책의 Appendix B에서 제시된 Reasoning / Logical Thinking의 틀을 숙지하여, 자신의 의견에 대한 근거를 항상 Practical / Psychological / Social한 면에서 구상하거나 (Rule #1), "More is better / new is better" (Rule #3), "Extreme is bad" (Rule #4) 등의 생각의 패턴을 활용할 준비를 하라. – 신속하게 생각을 정리하는 데 도움이 될 것이다.

그리고 두 개의 포인트면 충분하다는 것을 기억하라! 주어진 아주 짧은 시간에 설득력 있는 답을 하려면 너무 욕심을 내서는 안 된다.

3. 절대 답을 할 때 보고 '읽을' script를 준비하려고 하여서는 안 된다
답을 준비하는 시간이 15~30초로 절대적으로 부족하므로, 절대 답을 할 때 보고 '읽을' script를 준비하려고 하여서는 안 된다. 가능하지도 않고 또 어느 정도 한다고 해도 오히려 부자연스러운 답을 하게 될 수 있다. 대신 간략히 작성한 노트를 밑줄을 긋거나 번호를 매기면서 마음속에서 구도를 잡고 표현들을 빠르게 떠올려 놓는 것이 더 효과적이다.

4. As soon as your point makes sense, stop!
독립형 문제(Q1 & Q2)에서의 지시문에서 "use specific examples to support your answer"라고 나오지만 그것은 무시하는 것이 좋다. 45초의 시간은 세부적 보기를 들기에는 턱없이 부족하다. Examples보다는 간단한 explanations를 말한다고 생각하고 임하는 것이 더 완성도 있는 답을 하는 길이다. 보기를 드는 경우에는 에세이와는 달리 최소한의 detail만을 언급하라.

5. 완벽한 답보다는 전체적 Outline 또는 Summary를 전달한다

통합형 문제(Q3-Q6)에서도 완벽한 답보다는 전체적 outline 또는 summary를 전달한다는 마음으로 답을 구성하고 말하라. 대답에 주어지는 60초의 시간은 절대적으로 부족한 경우가 많다. 이러한 기본 태도를 갖지 않고 접근하면 말하는 중간에 녹음이 끊기는 경우가 발생하는데 이는 제대로 된 답을 구성하지 못했다는 인상을 남겨서 점수에 악영향을 끼친다. 차라리 세부 내용이 좀 부실하더라도 'completeness'가 느껴지는 답안이 더 완성도 높은, 그래서 또 고득점을 받을 수 있는 답이다.

6. 너무 화려하거나 세련된 표현을 생각하여 쓸 필요는 없다

마음에 바로 떠오르면 쓰지만 그렇지 않을 경우 무난한, 쉬운 표현을 쓰더라도 의미가 명확하게 전달되는 것이 더 효과적이다. 특히 통합형 문제에서는 integrated writing 과는 달리 paraphrasing을 최소화하는 것이 좋다. 잘 듣고 이해했는지, 그것을 다시 표현할 수 있는지가 평가되는 것이므로 conversations나 lectures에 나오는 표현을 그대로 사용하여 설명하여도 무방하다. 괜히 다른 표현으로 대체하려고 하다가 머뭇거리거나 쓸데없는 실수를 하는 것은 어리석은 것이다.

7. 자신만의 'Speaking Template'을 준비하라

자신만의 'Speaking Format / Template'을 만들어 항상 똑같은 표현으로 답의 골격을 유지하며 답을 하는 것이 좋다. 이렇게 하면 답에 대한 핵심 내용에 더 신경을 쓸 수 있고, 덜 머뭇거릴 수 있어 더 좋은 'delivery' 점수를 받을 수 있다. (매번 같은 표현을 써서 감점이 아닐까라는 논리적 우를 범하지 말기 바란다. 채점자 입장에서는 같은 표현이 아니라 적어도 당신으로부터는 처음 듣는 것이다!)

TOEFL-Speaking Template:

* 여기 나오는 표현들(또는 조금 변형된 자신만의 틀)을 완전히 외워서 실전에 활용하면 훨씬 더 안정되게 또 자신감 있게 답을 할 수 있을 것이다. 주의할 것은 이 template을 <u>대충 외워서는 효과가 없거나 오히려 부자연스럽게 답을 할 수도 있으니 자동적으로 나올 수 있도록 '완전히' 외워야 한다</u>는 것이다!
(SAT-Essay에서 template을 쓰는 경우보다 토플 스피킹에서는 performance적 요소가 상대적으로 더 많으므로 이러한 틀을 외워서 실전에 활용하면 정말 큰 차이를 낼 수 있다.)

#1 & 2

- Well, for me, (topic) is definitely/most certainly (your answer), there's no doubt. It ⋯
- Well, between the two given choices,
- I definitely prefer ⋯, because ⋯
- Well, I totally agree / disagree with the idea that ⋯
- Well, in my opinion, ⋯ include, ⋯

(Ending) So, that's my (answer) / So, for those reasons, that's my (answer/opinion/choice)

#3

- Well, according to the announcement / letter, ⋯
- Now, in response to this, the man/woman is
- ___ (x 2) definitely positive; he/she agrees! / definitely negative; he/she disagrees!

- Because, first, he/she points out that …
- Also, he/she indicates that …

(Ending) So, for those reasons, that's the man's/woman's opinion.

#4

- Well, according to the reading passage,
- (the concept) refers to (brief definition).
- Now, the professor in the lecture nicely
- (Q itself! – Use the expressions given in the question)

(Ending) So, those are the points given by the professor.

#5

- Well, the man's/woman's problem situation is that ---
- Now, in response to this, they are discussing two possible solutions to handle the situation. 1. _____. 2. _____.
- Now, in my opinion, 1st / 2nd option is clearly better, because 1. _____. 2. _____.
- Consider: Basic Courtesy/Basic duty of students / People don't change easily /+ or – consequences!

(Ending) (Optional: So, for those reasons, that's my choice of solution.)

#6

- Well, the professor in the lecture nicely

(Q itself! – Use the expressions given in the question)

(Ending) So, those are the points given by the professor.

TOEFL Speaking Sample
(위에서 제시된 Template을 적용한 사례이다.)

#1:

Well, for me, (the place that I go to often and it important for me) is definitely/most certainly (my school), there's no doubt. First of all, it is the place where I learn all the important skills for my future. For example, I am learning economics, and it is obviously something that I need for reaching my future career goal of becoming a successful businessman. Also, (it is where I have all my important friends, including my best friend. Through the interactions with them, I get to develop my communication skills, while cultivating important social networks, which will probably be very important for my future, too.)

+ So, that's my (answer)

#2:

Well, between the two given choices, I definitely (prefer the approach of taking variety of courses to get broad education in college, because, first of all, it is better in practical terms; I would be able to get ready for different jobs, which may be a major advantage in this fast changing, increasingly unpredictable world of globalization that we live in. Also, psychologically, it would be better in terms of the enjoyment that I can get during the processes; instead of getting bored by studying just one field, I can enjoy the sense of venturing into the unknown world of knowledge and skills.)

+ So, for those reasons, that's my opinion.

#3:

Well, according to the announcement, (the university has decided to eliminate the free bus service for the students.)

Now, in response to this, the man is definitely (negative; he disagrees!)

Because, first, he points out that (the bus routes are outdated; they don't go through the neighborhood where the students live, and if the university changes the routes, plenty of students will ride the buses.)

Also, he indicates that (stopping the bus service will encourage more students to drive on campus, and that will increase the noise. This will also increase the need for even more parking spaces).

+ So, for those reasons, that's the man's opinion.

#4:

Well, according to the reading passage, ('social influence') refers to (the impacts that people have on each other as they interact and perform certain tasks). Now, the professor in the lecture nicely (describes how the examples of tying shoes and learning to type demonstrate the principle of audience effect.) Audience effect is one kind of social influence; it is the effects of having others watch us when we perform certain tasks.

The first example was the case of two groups of students tying their shoe laces. One group thought that they are doing it alone, while the other group thought they are being watched. Those who thought that they are being watched tied their shoes faster, thus demonstrating the audience effect.

The second example was the cases of people learning something new, like learning how to type. When people thought that they are being watched, they typed faster, which was audience effect, too. Interestingly, they also made more mistakes along the way.

+ So, those are the points given by the professor.

#5:

Well, the woman's problem situation is that (she has a scheduling conflict situation. She can now go to the geology field trip since a student dropped out, but she already made a promise to help her history professor set up a museum exhibition).

Now, in response to this, they are discussing two possible solutions to handle the situation. First, she can ask the history professor to find a replacement, someone else to help her with the museum setup. Second is to finish helping the history professor before Wednesday which is the day of the trip). Now, in my opinion, the second option is clearly better, because, first of all, it is just the basic courtesy to keep the promise; she made a promise to the history professor, and it is just not right to break it at the last minute like this. Also, there will be a positive consequence of learning a lot from both; both the museum setup and the field trip can turn out to be very educational experiences for her.

+ Optional ending: So, for those reasons, that's my choice of solution.

#6:

Well, the professor in the lecture nicely (explains the two definitions of money, using respective examples).

The first is a 'broad' definition; money is anything that can be used to make purchases with. So, it includes the barter system. For example, when a taxi driver gives a ride to a farmer, he can get a five dollar bill, but he can get some vegetables from the farmer as a form of barter. The second one is a 'narrow' definition; money is something that is a legal tender in the society, whatever has to be accepted as a form of payment. So, in the same example, the taxi driver must accept a five dollar bill, but not the vegetable, since it is not a legal tender.

+ So, those are the points given by the professor.

TOEFL Writing 트레이너 Tips:

1. 충분히 brainstorm을 하고 outline 작성한 뒤 시작하라

일단 충분히 brainstorm과 outline을 하고 작성에 들어가라. 주어지는 시간의 약 4분의 1까지를 이 목적을 위해서 쓴다고 생각하면 된다. 일단 시작하고 보자는 식으로 타이핑을 시작하는 경우가 있는데 이는 바람직하지 않다. 그럴 경우 오히려 쓰는 중간중간에 우왕좌왕하게 되거나 아예 상당 부분을 다시 써야 하는 경우도 생기므로, 결국 더 많은 시간을 쓰게 됨을 기억하기 바란다. 잘 짜여진 outline은 실제 답안을 두 번 작성하는(고쳐 쓰는) 효과를 줄 수 있으며 좀 더 일관성 있는 글을 주어진 시간 내에 효율적으로 쓸 수 있게 해 준다.

2. 독립형 Essay는 길어야 점수가 잘 나온다

주어지는 시간이 20분 vs. 30분으로 되어 있다는 사실 자체로도 알 수 있지만, 일단 통합형 'Summary'와 독립형 'Essay'는 쓰는 양에 있어서 근본적으로 달라야 한다는 것을 기억하라! Summary는 말 그대로 '요약'을 하는 것이므로 간략하게 써야 한다. 그러나 필자의 수년간의 경험에 비추어 보면 Essay는 길어야 점수가 잘 나온다. 기본적으로 논리를 갖춘 에세이를 풍부한 세부 사항을 포함한 보기를 써서 충분히 '전개'(develop)시켜야 좋은 에세이가 되는 것이다. (통합형 250단어 전후 vs. 독립형 600단어 근접이 이상적이다.)

3. 통합형: listening passage(lecture)에 먼저 초점을 두어라

통합형 Summary 작성에서 일단 초점을 두어야 하는 부분은 listening passage (lecture) 부분이라는 것을 유의하라. – reading passage 부분이 먼저 나오고 또 작성하는 동안 다시 볼 수 있기 때문에 반대로 reading 부분에 초점을 두기 쉬운데, instruction을 잘 살펴보면 "Summarize the main points of the lecture you just heard, discussing how they cast doubt on the points in the reading passage" 라고 하는데, 이는 listening points가 main이 되어야 한다는 뜻이다. (출제 기관인 ETS에서 제공된 sample을 보더라도 이 점을 확인할 수 있다.) 그래서 lecture 부분의 각 포인트는 2-3sentences로 정리하고, 그에 해당하는 reading 부분 내용을 되도록 1sentence로 나타내는 것이 이상적이다. (Reading 또는 listening 부분 중 순서상 어느 것을 먼저 언급하는 것이 낫다는 룰은 없다. 둘 다 가능하지만 중요한 것은 listening 부분이 주가 되어 더 세부적으로 기술되어야 한다는 것이다.)

4. 통합형: 가능한 많이 paraphrasing 하라

Speaking 부분과는 달리 integrated writing에서는 가능한 한 많이 paraphrasing을 하라. 시간적으로 다른 표현으로 바꾸는 것이 가능한데, 그렇게 해야 주어진 내용의 뜻을 완전히 이해하였다는 것을 증명하는 것이며, 또한 vocabulary power를 보여주어 고득점의 가능성을 높일 수 있다. (그러나 생각나는 단어가 동의어인지 확신이 없을 때에는 그것을 써서 굳이 risk를 만들지 말고, 주어진 단어를 그대로 쓰는 것이 좋다.)

5. 독립형: 생각의 Rule을 활용하라

독립형 Essay 작성에 있어서는 speaking 부분과 마찬가지로 앞에 주어진 reasoning rule들을 활용하라. Speaking 부분에서 Rules #1과 #3를 활용하면 논리적 설득력이 있는 답을 작성하는 데 큰 도움이 된다. 의견에 대한 근거를 항상 Practical, Psychological, Social한 면에서 구상해 보라 – Writing에서도 두 가지 포인트면 충분하다는 것을 기억하라. – 하지만 3번째의 생각이 아주 compelling하게 마음에 떠올랐다면 그것까지 써서 3포인트를 가진 에세이를 작성할 수 있다!

6. 독립형: Intro. 부분에 너무 많은 시간을 할애하지 마라

독립형 Essay에서 intro. 부분의 작성에 너무 많은 시간을 할애하지 마라! 흔히들 intro.가 첫인상을 결정하기 때문에 중요하다고 생각하지만, 많은 경우의 채점자들은 사실 신경을 쓰지 않는 경우가 많다. 일단 '시험'이기 때문에, 어떤 주제에 대한 글인지 알기 때문에 'introduced' 될 필요가 없고, 또 진부한 표현이나 생각들이 많아서 경험이 쌓이다 보면 별로 신경을 쓰지 않게 된다. 그보다는 오히려 맨 마지막 끝 부분의 맺음말이라고 할 수 있는 'gift idea'(때로는 'kicker at the end'라고 불리는)가 더 중요하다. 아무래도 점수를 결정할 시간이 다가오면 자연스럽게 더 주의를 기울이는 게 채점자의 일반적인 심리다.

7. 독립형: Example을 되도록 길게 써라

독립형 답안은 통합형 답안과 달리 길게 쓸수록 좋다. (단, 같은 표현을 계속 반복하여서는 안 된다!) 물론 시간이 제한되어 있기 때문에 많은 학생들이 쉽게 할 수 있지는 않지만, 600단어에 근접하게 쓰는 것이 좋다. 이를 위해서 가장 효과적인 방법이 한 sub-topic(= reason)에 대하여 각각 두 개의 보기를, 그것도 최대한 세세한 detail을 포함하여 쓰는 것이 좋다. (이를 위하여 for example/for instance와 같은 진부한 표현보다는 이어서 주어지는 sample essay에 있는 보기를 소개하는 표현을 익혀 두면 유용할 것이다. e.g. the case of ~ sheds more light on this point; ~.)

8. 풍부한 어휘력을 과시하라

Speaking에서는 시간적 제한 때문에 권하지 않지만, writing에서는 되도록 많은 세련되고 독특한 표현을 생각하여 쓸수록 어휘력을 인정받을 수 있으므로 좋다. 그렇지만 표현이 적절히 생각나지 않을 경우 가장 기초적이고 쉬운 표현으로 대체하고 넘어가야지 너무 시간을 지체해서는 안 된다.

9. 자신만의 'Writing Format / Template'을 만들어라

Speaking에서 만큼 중요하지는 않지만, 자신만의 'Writing Format / Template'을 만들어 항상 같은 표현으로 글의 골격을 유지하며 작성하는 것이 좋다. 이렇게 하면 summary나 essay의 내용에 더 신경을 쓸 수 있고, 결국 더 설득력 있고 풍부한 내용을 가진 답안을 작성할 수 있다. (매번 같은 표현을 써서 감점이 아닐까라는 논리적 우를 범하지 말기 바란다. 채점자 입장에서는 Speaking과 마찬가지로 당신으로부터는 처음인 것이다! 그리고 막상 좀 진부하게 느껴진다 해도 틀리거나 어색한 표현을 즉흥적으로 사용하는 것보다는 그래도 낫다!)

10. 마지막 1분은 검토하는 시간으로 꼭 남겨 둘 것

Writing에서는 마지막 확인의 과정이 가능한데, 반드시 약 1분 30초, 최소 1분 정도는 시간을 남겨 두어 문법이나 용법의 실수가 없는지 확인하여야 한다. 작은 실수 한 개가 감점 요소는 아니지만 영어 실력에 대한 부정적 인상을 줄 수 있음으로 없어야 좋다. (이를 위하여 intro. 단락을 작성하고 그 다음 바로 concluding paragraph를 작성하는 습관을 들이는 것이 좋다. 이렇게 하면 마음의 안정감도 있어 더 일관성 있는 글을 쓰고 실수도 줄일 수 있다.)

TOEFL Writing Sample 1

⟨ Integrated Task ⟩

* 가장 중요한 것은 lecture 부분의 세부 사항을 다 적는 것이다. Recommended length가 225단어이지만 그걸 무시하고 보통 250~300단어 정도 적어야 나온 내용을 다 기술할 수 있다는 것을 기억하고 작성해야 content 점수를 다 받을 수 있음에 유의한다. (밑줄 친 부분은 Template으로 쓸 수 있는 표현들이다.)

Topic of the reading passage: ("The placebo effect is unreal and ineffective!")

Topic of the listening passage: ("The effect is real – not an illusion!")

Both the reading passage and the lecture are about topic of the placebo effect. **The professor in the lecture refutes the points given in the reading passage regarding** the unreal and ineffective aspects of it **by explaining the invalidating points involved.**

First of all, the patients show this effect only when they are aware of it, meaning that it is not something that happens naturally. It happens only when the patients are told about the anticipated effects and thus have expectations of them; when the patients have doubts, the effect is limited. **This is contrary to the point in the reading passage that** the effect is part of the natural healing processes that take place without any interventions.

In addition, the phenomenon is not just psychological but physically measurable as well. The brain scans of those who took fake painkillers showed increased amount of blood flow in their brains, indicating that the effect is actual. **This goes against the point in the reading passage that** it just involves feelings without any actually changes in the body.

Lastly, the effect is not always due to the changes in life-styles or exercise habits. As a proof, the professor cited the case of a Parkinson's disease patient who did not change any of his habits, but improved his symptoms when he took the placebo pills. **This differs from the reading**

part that the effect comes from the changes in the way the patients live when they go through treatments, rather than the placebos.

(Word count: 250)

TOEFL Writing Sample 2

빈도는 높지 않지만 가끔 Reading과 Listening 부분이 반대되는 경우가 아니고 Problem-Solution 형태로 연결되는 경우가 있으므로 주의해야 한다. "이러한 해결책이 있으므로 사실 문제가 아니다"라는 식의 frame으로 작성하면 반대의 내용으로 작성하는 것과 다르지 않으니 당황할 필요는 없고, 다만 표현을 다음의 샘플에서 있는 것을 기억하고 접근하면 좋다.

⟨ Integrated Task⟩

Topic of the reading passage: ("The problems and difficulties of dealing with the global warming phenomenon!")

Topic of the listening passage: ("The solutions for the stated problems!")

Both the reading passage and the lecture are about the topic of the global warming problem. **The professor in the lecture discusses the points given in the reading passage regarding** the problematic aspects of the phenomenon **by explaining possible solutions for them**.

To begin with, spending money to improve the production and waste management techniques now will result in much greater savings in the long run. Despite the huge costs needed, not giving up short term profits is unwise and could eventually result in the fall of the world's economy, which will make any savings meaningless. **This is offered as the solution to the point in the reading passage that** the costs of taking care of global warming are tremendously burdensome and increasing rapidly.

Secondly, taking action now to prevent or reverse erosions in the coastal areas will prevent the loss of space for populations and the natural habitats of many species affected by the melting of glaciers. Also, efforts to stop the loss of alpine glaciers need to continue. **This addresses the problem indicated in the reading passage that** higher sea levels cause coastal erosions, resulting in less usable land for humans and animals.

Lastly, national governments and international health organizations must implement measures to prevent the health risks linked with global warming. Some simple and relatively cheap methods can be taken to reduce heat stress for people and animals. **This is the point discussed as the solution for the problem mentioned in the reading part that** global warming presents numerous health threats, most significantly heat stress.

(Word count: 258)

TOEFL Writing Sample 3

〈 Independent Task〉

Topic: "Co-workers are the people who work with us together. In your opinion, **what are the qualities of a good co-worker?**"

(전형적으로 Rule #1 – Practical, Psychological, Social로 생각을 분류해서 그중 두 가지에 대하여 기술할 수 있는 경우이다. 어떤 중요한 요소나 조건 등을 묻는 주제의 경우 그러한 변수가 있으면 좋은 점뿐 아니라 없을 경우 어떤 결과가 있을지에 대하여도 기술하면 깊이 있게 잘 develop된 에세이가 나올 수 있다는 점을 기억하면서 살펴보기 바란다.)

(Sample Essay)

Rarely anyone would deny the importance of co-workers in our life; besides family and friends, they are probably the ones who affect us most. I strongly believe that there are mainly two qualities on coworkers that make them good ones to work with: professional competence and considerateness.

To begin with, in practical terms, one must be professionally competent to be a good coworker. In other words, s/he has to be knowledgeable and skilled in the given area in order to be a good person to work with. This is important in two aspects.

One is simply the achievement; if one is capable in the field, s/he will be helpful in getting things done efficiently and successfully, and that means accomplishing the tasks as needed. For instance, my mother is a software developer and she has a very experienced and professional co-worker. On numerous occasions, she told me how her coworker was critical in finishing projects successfully by the deadlines, and thus getting positive performance evaluations as a team. Another aspect is the learning that is possible when you work with a competent co-worker. In an automotive repair shop setting, for example, working with an experienced and capable coworker would be similar to having a good mentor; you would learn a lot from that person and improve your own ability as times goes by. However, if your coworker lacks professional abilities, working with that person would probably bring numerous occasions in which delays and failures will occur, with frequent experiences of getting frustrated or even angry. Thus, ability does matter a lot in a coworker

Furthermore, in emotional terms, another important factor that would make a person a good coworker is her/his considerateness. A person who is always considerate about others' situations and and emotionally sensitive to the needs of the co-workers would make the processes of working together with that person a joyful experience. My cousin who works as a paralegal (legal assistant) at a law firm has a perfect example of a co-worker with this quality. My cousin is a working mother, and she experiences many 'unexpected' situations in which she has to cater to the need of my niece who is a 1st grader, which means that she has to take a leave of absence more frequently than

most others. Fortunately, her co-worker who also works at the office as a paralegal is a very sensitive person who understands how difficult it can be for a working mother to take care of matters related kids. So, when my cousin has to come to work late or leave early, she understands and offers to take care of some of the my cousin's work, making it possible to manage her duties and reducing anxiety and stress. In some settings, having inconsiderate coworkers can mean extreme stress and anxiety about the job, and some people may even choose to quit their jobs because of the insensitivity of the coworkers.

Hence, the two aforementioned qualities of competence and considerateness are the crucial characteristics that would make a person an ideal partner at workplaces. Recognizing the importance of those qualities and trying to be those ways ourselves would be a wise idea for anyone who wishes to have pleasant job experiences.

(Word count: 547)

TOEFL Writing Sample 4

⟨ Independent Task⟩

Topic: "Do you agree or disagree with the following statement? **Playing games teaches us much about life.**"

(일상적인 주제로 찬-반 양쪽 모두 비교적 쉽게 생각할 수 있는 주제이다. 양쪽이 비슷하게 쉽다면 예를 들 수 있는 사항들을 빠르게 생각한 뒤 더 설득력 있을 것 같은 방향을 'more and new is usually better'라는 판단의 틀을 써서 결정한다(Reasoning Rule #3). 근거를 제시할 때 역시 Rule #1 - Practical, Psychological, Social을 사용하여 생각을 분류한 후 그중 두 가지에 대하여 기술할 수 있는 경우이다. 분량이 적다고 느껴질 경우 추가적 예를 제시하여 늘릴 수 있다. 여기서는 찬성 및 반대 입장에서 각각 샘플을 제시하여 본다. 찬성의 경우 본문에 세 가지 포인트로 구성을 하였는데, 보통 두 가지인 경우도 충분하지만 세 개의 포인트가 비교적 쉽게 생각이 나서 쓴다면 contents 점수를 잘 받을 수 있음을 기억하기 바란다.)

(Sample Essay 4A - Agree!)

Playing games is undeniably an important element of our living experiences. Some people might say that games are just for fun, but I agree with the statement that "games teach us much about life", considering practical, emotional, and interpersonal factors involved.

In practical terms, games often expose us to concepts and theories that are quite relevant and informative about various situations that we encounter in life. The game of 'Monopoly' can serve as a perfect example here. It is a game that lets people engage in various real-estate related situations, and thus allows people to get 'indirect' experiences in buying, renting, or mortgaging properties. People can get familiarized with the concepts like mortgage in the processes of playing the game, which can be helpful later when they contemplate buying a house in real life. Sports games in general can also be taken as good examples in support of the statement given. We have to abide by the rules when we play sports games, and we have to beat the opponents in competitions to attain some positions of distinction, which are quite similar to many the real life situations of school or work settings.

Furthermore, emotionally, games can provide us with wonderful learning opportunities. The virtue of hard work and persistence can be learned through the processes of practicing to play many sports games. Then, the fact that we cannot win every game, and thus we need to recognize our limits and sometimes sadly give up our lofty goals or dreams, can all be learned through playing games. Even the qualities of anger control and humbleness can be learned through various games. For instance, when I was in grade school, I used to play the oriental board game 'Go' as part of he my school's club activities, and I realized that getting angry at my loss does not help at all; I learned that I need to control my anger in order to think right and eventually win. Oftentimes, games present us diverse situations in which the variety of human emotions can be experienced and controlled, including the joys, frustrations, and humility.

Last but not least, games can teach us a lot about social knowledge and skills. Most games involve human interactions and that often means chances to learn how to communicate and interact with others. Again, various sports games like baseball can serve as prime examples. When we play baseball, we have to communicate with our coaches and teammates regarding the strategies involved. Sometimes, a failure to communicate can result in stupid errors being made, costing the entire game. We even have to communicate with other members outside the field and in the locker room; we may have to communicate with others in arranging the practice sessions and in the processes of building the sense of cooperation and unity. When we think about the fact that, in college application processes, students' records in athletics are often considered in the applicant's favor, the educational values of playing sports games become even more obvious.

Hence, when the above explained factors related to playing games are taken into consideration, the given idea that games teach us much about life becomes undeniably convincing. It will be wise for us to keep these points in mind and try to take advantage of numerous educational opportunities that games can offer us in life.

(Word count: 557)

(Sample Essay 4B - Disagree!)

When we consider all the amount of time that we spend in playing games, it can indeed be said that games are important part of our life. Some people argue that playing games teaches us about life. However, I disagree with the view, based on the fact that they are simplified and that people don't take them as occasions of enjoyment.

To begin with, in practical terms, games are not as complex as our life. They involve simplified versions of life situations that are not quite the same. In fact, many of the conditions in games are unrealistic or exaggerated. For instance, the simple fact that sports games always have clear win vs. lose results can illustrate this; in real life, it is not so simple and thus we cannot clearly identify winners and losers; there are many instances in which the results are win-win or lose-lose for both of the parties involved, like in cases of sibling rivalry or fights between boyfriends and girlfriends. Sports games in general can also be taken as examples; rarely do situations in life have lines to tell whether a move or ball is inside or outside, and there are often cases where we have to settle disputes by ourselves, rather than having definitive calls from referees. Many events in life unfold in ways that we do not and cannot expect; there are complicated and sometimes unpredictable variables that affect the results in ways that are quite often not in the direction of what is expected or desired. These can be taken as indications that what we learn from games are quite limited in terms of their applicability in real life settings.

Furthermore, in an emotional sense, games are taken as fun occasions by people, and thus serious learning cannot really take place. Since people are aware of the fact that they are for fun and not 'real' what they people experience in game-playing situations will not translate into learning. To illustrate, the case of playing the board game "Monopoly" can be considered. The game involves many concepts in 'real life' real estate investments and transactions. However, since people know it is 'just a game,' people don't take the situation seriously and thus not much learning takes place; they just have good times with friends and family, but they do not really think that they are buying or renting properties for real. The way we spend money and make investment decisions are quite different from how we think and what we do when we play the game of monopoly for fun with friends and family. Therefore, what we gain from games cannot be deemed highly educational about life.

Hence, for the two reasons aforementioned with examples about games, I stand on the con side of the statement that games teach us much about life. This should not, however, be misunderstood as saying that games are totally useless; of course, if we play them for the right occasions and for the right purposes, they can be valuable, especially in a psychological sense.

(Word count: 508)

Appendix D

연습용 답안(복사용)지

(실제 시험 답지보다 25% 정도 작은 이 책의 크기로 보아 여기 주어진 답지로 연습할 경우 대략 3~3.5페이지--대략 700단어 전후 - 정도의 분량으로 작성하는 연습을 하면 이상적이다.)

SAT-Essay-Practice Answer Sheet

Grading Standards: Your Name: _____

Reading: (score range: 2 - 8): _____

Did the student demonstrate full comprehension of the reading passage given?

(The purpose / kind of passage / sub-topics, etc.)

Analysis: (score range: 2 - 8): _____

Did the student correctly identify and indicate the strategies, reasoning, and styles used by the author of the passage?

(Citing specific data, referring to authorities, personification, allusion, etc.)

Writing: (score range: 2 - 8): _____

Did the student demonstrate his/her command of English in writing the essay?

(Correct grammar and usage, the right choices of words, adequate structure of the essay, etc.)